"This is an excellent, systematic, helpful, and practical workbook. Doing these practices brings many blessings. They will reduce your stress and truly transform your life."

—Jack Kornfield, Ph.D., author of *The Wise Heart*, *A Path with Heart*, and *After the Ecstasy, the Laundry*

"Bob Stahl and Elisha Goldstein have woven an inspiring tapestry of illuminating insights and practical exercises that can transform your life and even help you build a stronger brain. Inspired by their work as teachers of the research-proven Mindfulness-Based Stress Reduction Program, the authors have provided a step-by-step approach to bringing this scientifically grounded approach into your daily life. Mindfulness has been demonstrated to effectively help us live with less stress, fear, and anxiety and to cultivate more ease, connection, and well-being in our lives. This workbook makes mindfulness understandable and offers a carefully laid-out plan to achieve a healthier and more meaningful life. There is no time like the present to bring these pearls and practices of wisdom into your life. Why not start now?"

—Daniel J. Siegel, MD, codirector of the University of California, Los Angeles Mindful Awareness Research Center and author of *Mindsight* and *The Mindful Brain*

"In their wonderful new book, Bob Stahl and Elisha Goldstein have provided each reader with wise, clear, step-by-step guidance for cultivating a personal mindfulness practice and for applying the resulting awareness to the stress and challenges of living. This workbook is a perfect companion to Jon Kabat-Zinn's well-known book, *Full Catastrophe Living*, which is the foundation text for all mindfulness-based stress reduction courses."

—Jeffrey Brantley, MD, DFAPA, director of the Mindfulness-Based Stress Reduction Program at Duke Integrative Medicine

"I found this workbook informative, helpful, and user-friendly. It is filled with pragmatic tools to keep the practitioner on track and would be beneficial to all who read it."

—Sharon Salzberg, author of *Lovingkindness*, *A Heart as Wide as the World*, and *Faith*

"This fine book is about the unburdening of the mind and the release of our inherent wisdom. It breaks the hard sternum of our resistance and opens the lotus of the heart. The method that ends our madness."

—Stephen Levine, author of *Who Dies?*, *A Year to Live*, and *Unattended Sorrow*

"We are such a stressed society that many of us are stressed about how stressed we are. Books abound that give us more information. But *A Mindfulness-Based Stress Reduction Workbook* takes a far more helpful approach. It takes you by the hand and leads you step by step. If you want your life to have greater balance and peace, if you want to live with less stress and more joy, I can't recommend this beautiful offering highly enough."

—John Robbins, author of *Healthy at 100, Diet for a New America,* and *Reclaiming Our Health*

"The biggest challenge for any do-it-yourself course is to include exercises that people will actually want to stop and do. In this book, the exercises are skillfully introduced along with spaces that remind the reader, 'This part is up to you to do now!' I think readers will start practicing immediately with confidence that the program will show results."

—Sylvia Boorstein, author of *Happiness Is an Inside Job, It's Easier than You Think,* and *That's Funny, You Don't Look Buddhist*

"This book is an excellent guide to the life-changing practice of mindfulness. In these pages, you will find the missing piece, the hidden truth, and the open secret. Mindfulness saved my life and transformed my world. This workbook offers the key to health, happiness and freedom. Read it, work it, practice it, and be free."

—Noah Levine, MA, author of *Dharma Punx* and *Against the Stream*

"What a delight it has been to review this beautifully written, deeply important book that offers readers a path toward a new life balance. For those interested in knowing more about what it is that has excited so many in the fields of medicine, psychology, neuroscience, and education, this book is a mind-opening volume that will clarify the key concepts of mindful meditation. Those who simply want to find ways to reduce stress and anxiety will find it to be an extraordinary aid. Those in a program of mindfulness-based stress reduction will find this book an invaluable addition to their training. *A Mindfulness-Based Stress Reduction Workbook* adds depth to the practice of mindfulness for everyone, from beginning practitioners to experienced teachers of mindfulness stress reduction classes."

—Marion Solomon, Ph.D., director of training at the Lifespan Learning Institute and author of *Love and War in Intimate Relationships*

"This book, along with the CD giving mindfulness meditation guided sessions, provides an excellent overview of how the practice of mindfulness can be a very effective stress reduction intervention."

—G. Alan Marlatt, Ph.D., professor and director of the Addictive Behaviors Research Center at the University of Washington

"Bob Stahl and Elisha Goldstein's *A Mindfulness-Based Stress Reduction Workbook* is a practical, user-friendly guide to mindfulness meditation and stress reduction. If you feel that your life is spinning out of control and you can't get perspective, if you are moving too fast and don't know how to slow down, or if you are starting to have health problems related to stress, this program—which includes an excellent companion CD and access to an innovative online community— is for you. I am thrilled that this clarity, compassion, and wisdom will be available to a greater audience through this exceptional, life-changing guide."

—Laura Davis, author of *The Courage to Heal* and *I Thought We'd Never Speak Again*

"This is an incredible resource for anyone who is interested in reducing stress in their lives. We all live in a world where it is easy to feel overwhelmed and discouraged. This workbook and the accompanying audio program is the best resource I know of for helping us stay present and centered when so many forces would push us off balance. I highly recommend it for clients, fellow professionals, and any man or woman who wants to have more comfort, ease, and joy in their lives."

—Jed Diamond, Ph.D., author of *The Irritable Male Syndrome* and *Male Menopause*

"For anyone drawn to a path of mindfulness, this workbook will provide a clear and accessible companion. Authors Bob Stahl and Elisha Goldstein expertly guide readers through a rich assortment of mindfulness practices and reflections, providing invaluable tools for handling stress and living life with presence and heart."

—Tara Brach, Ph.D., author of *Radical Acceptance*

"Bob Stahl and Elisha Goldstein have done a superb job bringing the cultivation of mindfulness to life in their excellent workbook. This workbook is a tremendous resource for those wanting to develop greater health, vitality, and peace. I highly recommend it."

—Shauna L. Shapiro, Ph.D., coauthor of *The Art and Science of Mindfulness*

"A workbook perfectly poised between the promise and practice of MBSR. Replete with clinical wisdom and helpful practices, this workbook illustrates how mindful engagement with the inevitable stresses in our lives can temper their impact on our minds and bodies."

—Zindel Segal, Ph.D., author of *The Mindful Way Through Depression*

A
Mindfulness-Based
Stress Reduction
Workbook

BOB STAHL, PH.D.
ELISHA GOLDSTEIN, PH.D.

New Harbinger Publications, Inc.

Publisher's Note

This publication is designed to provide accurate and authoritative information in regard to the subject matter covered. It is sold with the understanding that the publisher is not engaged in rendering psychological, financial, legal, or other professional services. If expert assistance or counseling is needed, the services of a competent professional should be sought.

The recommendations made in this workbook are generic and are not meant to replace formal medical or psychiatric treatment. Individuals with medical or psychological problems should consult with their physician or therapist about following the program in this workbook and discuss appropriate modifications relevant to their unique circumstances and conditions. Lastly, in writing this workbook, we have tried our best to be as accurate as possible. If there are any misrepresentations, they are from us and not from the rich teachings of mindfulness.

Distributed in Canada by Raincoast Books

Copyright © 2010 by Bob Stahl & Elisha Goldstein
New Harbinger Publications, Inc.
5674 Shattuck Avenue
Oakland, CA 94609
www.newharbinger.com

FSC
Mixed Sources
Product group from well-managed
forests and other controlled sources
Cert no. SW-COC-002283
www.fsc.org
© 1996 Forest Stewardship Council

Acquired by Catharine Sutker; Cover design by Amy Shoup; Edited by Nelda Street; Text design by Tracy Carlson

Library of Congress Cataloging-in-Publication Data

Stahl, Bob.
  A mindfulness-based stress reduction workbook / by Bob Stahl and Elisha Goldstein.
      p. cm.
  Includes bibliographical references.
  ISBN 978-1-57224-708-6
  1. Stress management. 2. Stress (Psychology) I. Goldstein, Elisha. II. Title.
  RA785.S73 2009
  616.9'8--dc22

                                    2009051814

13 12 11
10 9 8 7 6 5 4

What lies behind us and what lies before us are small matters compared to what lies within us.

—Ralph Waldo Emerson

To all those who have dared to look into their fears and find their hearts.

contents

❋ **chapter 1** ❋
what is mindfulness?

❋ **chapter 2** ❋
mindfulness and the mind-body connection

❋ **chapter 3** ❋
how to practice mindfulness meditation

❋ **chapter 4** ❋
how mindfulness works with stress reduction

foreword

Dear Reader:

There are many different and complementary descriptors that might be used to characterize this precious and exceedingly useful offering you have in your hands. Its title suggests that it is a workbook, and it is certainly that. It invites us into and guides us through a potentially profound and healing undertaking, one that involves, even requires, significant personal commitment and an ongoing fidelity of engagement. This is precisely what mindfulness teachers mean when speaking of interior discipline. The ultimate fidelity, of course, is to yourself—to your very life, your moments, and the beauty of your being, even if you don't always see it or even know it is here. It is humbling to think that being present and nonjudgmental is perhaps the hardest work in the world, and the most necessary. All the more reason for us to undertake it wholeheartedly. Our very lives and even the well-being of the world, in ways both small and large, may hang in the balance.

But it would be good if you could also think of this book as a *playbook*, because mindfulness is really a playful adventuring within life itself. The discipline required needs to be taken on as much in the spirit of play as in the spirit of hard work, for it is both. Mindfulness and the curriculum and challenges of MBSR and of life itself, and perhaps your reasons for picking up this book in the first place, are far too serious to take too seriously. The play element invites us to approach everything, especially when being guided by the formal meditation instructions, with the lightest of touches, and to not take ourselves too seriously, or fall into idealizing either the process itself or the imagined and hoped-for outcomes of MBSR training, even though your motivation for coming to this engagement, and the personal stakes in terms of its potential benefits for you, are serious indeed.

You are certainly in very good hands in this undertaking. Bob Stahl and Elisha Goldstein sound just the right notes here, cognitively, emotionally, relationally, somatically. Even though we are not in the classroom together with them week by week in a literal sense, in a larger way, we definitely are, or can be if we throw ourselves into the work and the play of the text and its reflections, suggestions, and written exercises, and make regular and good use of the guided mindfulness practices on the accompanying

CD, whether or not we feel like it on any given day. We can benefit enormously from their welcoming hospitality, their invitation to participate fully to whatever degree we can manage, and their warmth as teachers and as people. Their warmth emanates off each page and from every practice track on the CD, reminding us in the very feeling of it of the overriding need for us to honor ourselves and embrace our experience with kindness and compassion, not in an inflated or ego-enhancing sense, but rather in the true and matter-of-fact sense of seeing and acknowledging ourselves as worthy and whole, just by virtue of being human, no matter how convinced we may be of our shortcomings and inadequacies. The authors know, and you can feel it in these pages, that all of us are, when it comes right down to it, miraculous beings, with unimaginable potential for learning, growing, healing, and transformation across the life span; that we are much larger than who we think we are; and that we are perfect as we are, including all the ways in which we know that we are imperfect.

Have you ever wondered whether that aspect of your being that is aware of your shortcomings itself suffers from those or even any shortcomings? Or whether your awareness of pain when you feel pain is actually in pain? Or if your awareness of your fear, at times when it might arise, is afraid? This is something you can actually investigate, and see for yourself, especially at key moments when you *do* feel overwhelmed by feelings of inadequacy, or by pain or fear, or by any other experience. There are whole new hidden dimensions of being and of experience to discover and inhabit here in this laboratory of our lives unfolding moment by moment, in this adventure in embodying that which is deepest and best in ourselves, which is already here and so does not need to be "gotten," and which we have perhaps ignored for most of our lives—the faculty we call awareness, which is mysteriously and seamlessly both mind and heart.

Mindfulness involves an elemental and spontaneous openness to experience, grounded in the body, in the timeless, in not expecting anything to happen, a befriending and inhabiting of this present moment for its own sake. When you rest in mindful awareness, you are participating intimately in life as it is unfolding, seeing what happens, experimenting, allowing the original beauty and mystery of the world and of yourself to speak to you, without shying away from wonder, and awe, and joy—and the miracle of being alive in these precious present moments that are available to all of us but that we so often ignore in the hope of some "better" ones at some future time.

This volume is a playbook in another sense as well: it is a collection of well-thought-out strategies and exercises for navigating your relationship to the twists and turns and ups and downs of life, and the various challenges and obstacles that inevitably arise over the course of a day, or a lifetime, in this increasingly unpredictable and stressful world. These are practices that have been utilized by human beings for millennia, and that have been demonstrated to be effective both in clinical environments and in the laboratory over the past thirty plus years, during which time mindfulness has become an intimate part of modern medicine and health care in many different and continually expanding ways (Krasner et al. 2009; Ludwig and Kabat-Zinn 2008; Didonna 2008).

You can also think of the text as a supreme cookbook—but not in the usual sense of a compilation of recipes that you can just follow and get a delicious result, because each page and each exercise is missing the most critical ingredient: you. The meals offered up in the form of mindfulness practices and the entire curriculum of mindfulness-based stress reduction are potentially lifesaving and life transforming. However, this book cannot perform its magic until you throw yourself into the pot of mindfulness and begin cooking yourself. You are at the same time the recipe and the meal and the cook; the authors your loyal and caring sous-chefs. You can regulate the heat according to your capacity at any given time, in order to modulate your engagement as appropriate. When you show up completely in any moment, the practices within these pages come alive. You may discover that they will stand you in good stead and wake you up in all your moments to the possibilities of healing, self-compassion, and compassion for others within even the darkest and most difficult of circumstances.

Speaking of mystery and miracles for a moment, recent research has shown that our human brain is an organ that is continually changing not only its function but also its structure on the basis of experience, and in particular, repetitive experience over extended periods of time. This discovery of an inherent plasticity in brain architecture and function, known as *neuroplasticity*, implies that what we call the mind actually shapes the brain, and drives transformation of our intrinsic capacities, and it does so not just in childhood but across our entire life span.[1] If the repetitive experiences are traumatic in nature, it can lead to actual shrinking in parts of the brain, and diminished mental and social capacity. This can happen due to physical injury to the brain itself, or due to repeated emotional trauma in childhood or adulthood that can lead to depressive and dissociative syndromes and disordered social relations and behaviors. Happily, there is also compelling evidence that interventions based on repetitive positive experience may be restorative and therapeutic. Exercise itself, which tends to be highly repetitive when engaged in regularly, is a major driver of neuroplastic changes in the brain, which is why physical exercise is one of the most important factors in restoring and maintaining mental as well as physical health across the life span, starting from the moment one begins such a program. Increasing evidence from laboratory studies of meditators has shown that the repetitive practices at the heart of meditative disciplines can drive positive neuroplastic changes that also reflect mental and physical well-being, such as greater emotional balance, compassion, and genuine happiness, as well as a potential buffering of stressful and traumatic experience when it does occur (Lutz, Dunne, and Davidson 2007).

So the mind can change the brain (Siegel 2007; Begley 2008). This means that if we train our minds through meditative disciplines such as MBSR, we can grow into seeing more clearly and acting spontaneously with greater awareness, compassion, and wisdom. And since what we call mind is not separate from what we call heart, we can speak of mindfulness and heartfulness as complementary aspects of MBSR. What is more, since we cannot speak of mind or brain without a body, the core of this work, as you shall see, includes befriending your body with gentleness and acceptance, however it is in any moment. This in itself can be a major attitudinal challenge for anyone who might feel betrayed by his or her body and very much in need of befriending it or re-befriending it. Realizing that, as the authors emphasize, "as long as you are breathing, there is more right with you (and your body) than there is wrong with you" in any given moment makes for a very good place to begin. We can trust in the process, we can trust the expertise of Bob and Elisha, and above all, we can place our trust in our own capacity to pay attention in new ways and learn and grow from this attending.

Mindfulness is the container that holds it all. Therefore, your commitment to practice is what is most important here—and, paradoxically, your willingness to engage in practice for its own sake, to be in touch with life unfolding, however it is in any given moment, yet without being too attached to attaining any outcome. This is at the core of the invitation to enter into this engagement with an open mind

---

1 Even as the physical, material brain in our cranium, of course, allows for the phenomenon we call "mind," including the ability of the mind to experience and know itself.

and an open heart, without necessarily thinking you know what you will get out of it, and committing yourself anyway—a gesture of faith in yourself and your truest possibilities, which are always unknown. Ultimately, as we shall come to see, life itself is the real teacher, and how we meet it moment by moment the real meditation practice.

So now, it is time to roll up our sleeves, and begin.

I wish you all the best in this adventure of a lifetime.

—Jon Kabat-Zinn
October 1, 2009

References

Begley, S. 2008. *Train Your Mind, Change Your Brain: How a New Science Reveals Our Extraordinary Potential to Transform Ourselves*. New York: Ballantine Books.

Didonna, F. 2008. *Clinical Handbook of Mindfulness*. New York: Springer.

Krasner, M. S., R. M. Epstein, H. Beckman, A. L. Suchman, B. Chapman, C. J. Mooney, and T. E. Quill. 2009. Association of an educational program in mindful communication with burnout, empathy, and attitudes among primary care physicians. *Journal of the American Medical Association* 302 (12): 1338–40.

Ludwig, D. S. and J. Kabat-Zinn. 2008. Mindfulness in medicine. *Journal of the American Medical Association* 300 (11): 1350–2.

Lutz, A, J. D. Dunne, R. J. Davidson. 2007. Meditation and the neuroscience of consciousness: An introduction. In *The Cambridge Handbook of Consciousness*, edited by P. D. Zelazo, M. Moscovitch, and E. Thompson. Cambridge, UK: Cambridge University Press.

Siegel, D. J. 2007. *The Mindful Brain: Reflections and Attunement in the Cultivation of Well-Being*. New York: Norton.

acknowledgments

I'd like to acknowledge my parents Marilyn and Alvan Stahl, who gave me the gift of life and unconditional love. They taught me that we aren't islands; we're connected to all beings. I want to express endless gratitude to my wife, Jan Landry, and our two sons, Ben and Bodhi, who have been my greatest teachers and loved and supported me through and through. I also give thanks for all the love and support from my brother, Barry, and sister, Kim, and their families. Endless gratitude to my grandparents, Netti and Ben, Ida and Samuel, who taught me kindness and levity and seeded so much love into all of our families. I also want to express my boundless homage to my beloved meditation teachers Taungpulu Sayadaw, Hlaing Tet Sayadaw, Pakokku Sayadaw, and Dr. Rina Sircar. I wouldn't be on this mindful path without them. Much gratitude to my beloved dharma friends Mary Grace Orr, Steve Flowers, Skip Regan, Melissa Blacker, Florence Meleo-Meyer, Tom Williams, Jon Kabat-Zinn, and Saki Santorelli, who continue to inspire and support me in this wondrous path of wisdom and compassion, and also to my MBSR teacher colleagues in Northern California and at the Center for Mindfulness at the University of Massachusetts Medical School. I also want to acknowledge the thousands of students I've had the honor of working with through the years, who have humbled me and helped me grow to become a better person and teacher.

Many bows to Elisha Goldstein, my compadre and cowriter. Elisha is a very kind and wise man, and I have learned much from him. It has been such a gift to write this book with him and deeply honor our collaborations and friendship.

—Bob

I'd like to express my love and gratitude to my wife, Stefanie, who continues to show me the path of interpersonal mindfulness and inspires me daily. I would also like to thank the new addition to my family, my son, Lev, who reminds me of beginners mind and becoming present on a daily basis. I want to express appreciation for my parents, Jan, Jane, Steve, and Bonnie, and their unwavering belief in me. My sisters, Yaffa, Batsheva, and Shira, and brother, Ari, have also been a tremendous source of inspiration and love. I'm grateful to my in-laws, Judy and George Nassif, and to Audrey and Karl Jacobs for their encouragement, love, and support. Last but not least in respect to family, I'd like to thank my cats, Shechinah and Mr. Butternut, who have spent endless hours on my lap keeping me company while I was writing this book.

I also want to extend many thanks to Trudy Goodman and Christiane Wolf, at InsightLA, for their friendship, support, and wise guidance, and to fellow teacher and kindred spirit Roger Nolan. In addition, it has been my privilege to teach and be taught by all of the students and patients who have allowed me into their lives.

It has been a true blessing to walk this path with Bob Stahl. Bob is not only an insightful teacher, but a wise man with an awakened heart. Writing this book together has been such a meaningful process, and I'm grateful for his friendship and support.

—Elisha

We want to thank our first editor, John Malkin, who helped launch this journey, as well editors Jess O'Brien, Jess Beebe, Jasmine Star, and Troy DuFrene at New Harbinger, who helped us make this book the best book it can be. Big gratitude to dharma brother Skip Regan, who mastered the audio recordings CD for our workbook. Deep thanks to Karen Zelin, who posed for the yoga illustrations, and to Bill Underwood and Ben Stahl, who did the photography that the illustrations are based on. Many thanks to our agent, Stephanie Tade, who is compassionate, wise, and savvy in guiding us in the world of publishing.

Thank you to the following people who helped shape this book or gave us important feedback: Jon Kabat-Zinn, Dan Siegel, Melissa Blacker, Steve Flowers, Richard Davidson, Sara Lazar, Bruce Eisendorf, Ed Plonka, Karen Zelin, Jason Ong, Janetti Marotta, Stefanie Goldstein, Jan Landry, Susan Chamberlain, Tom Lane, Ivan Sokolov, Nancy Gill, Celeste Baross, Patti Breitman, B. Jane Wick, Steve Nelson, Jan Goldstein, and Bonnie Goldstein.

Much appreciation to our colleagues who have supported and endorsed our book: Jack Kornfield, Sharon Salzberg, Tara Brach, Stephen Levine, Sylvia Boorstein, John Robbins, Noah Levine, Marion Solomon, G. Alan Marlatt, Shauna Shapiro, Laura Davis, Dan Siegal, and Jed Diamond. We extend especially deep gratitude and respect to Jon Kabat-Zinn and Saki Santorelli for their profound contributions in bringing mindfulness into medicine, health, and society. We honor their commitment to integrity, wisdom, and compassion. They are the embodiment of walking the talk, and their vision, leadership, and practice have had a tremendous effect on us both personally and professionally.

—Bob and Elisha

introduction

Welcome to *A Mindfulness-Based Stress Reduction Workbook*. We thank you for purchasing this workbook and want to fully affirm that in doing so you're taking an active role in your health and well-being. If you're feeling any signs or symptoms of stress, such as anxiety, irritability, muscle tension, burnout, apathy, restlessness, headaches, fatigue, stomach distress, difficulty in concentrating, worry, overwork, substance abuse, smoking, eating problems, sleep disturbances, or feeling overwhelmed, this workbook can help. It can also help with the stresses associated with living with illness, chronic pain, and conditions such as AIDS, arthritis, asthma, cancer, fibromyalgia, gastrointestinal disorders, heart disease, high blood pressure, migraines, and many other medical conditions.

Simply put, mindfulness is the practice of cultivating nonjudgmental awareness in day-to-day life. This educational and experiential workbook will introduce you to mindfulness meditation and teach you simple, profound practices that can decrease suffering and bring you greater balance and peace. You'll find that these tools help you maximize your life and experience, even in the midst of stress, pain, and illness.

As an affirmation of the healing path you're embarking upon, we'd like to dedicate the following poem by Mary Oliver to you:

One day you finally knew
what you had to do, and began,
though the voices around you
kept shouting
their bad advice—
though the whole house
began to tremble
and you felt the old tug
at your ankles.

"Mend my life!"
each voice cried.
But you didn't stop.
You knew what you had to do,
though the wind pried
with its stiff fingers
at the very foundations—
though their melancholy
was terrible.
It was already late
enough, and a wild night,
and the road full of fallen
branches and stones.
But little by little,
as you left their voices behind,
the stars began to burn
through the sheets of clouds,
and there was a new voice,
which you slowly
recognized as your own,
that kept you company
as you strode deeper and deeper
into the world,
determined to do
the only thing you could do—
determined to save
the only life you could save.

—Mary Oliver, "The Journey" (1992, 14)

the human condition

Despite considerable research into stress and anxiety and seemingly innumerable approaches to stress management and reduction, stress is an unavoidable fact of life. It's the human condition and always has been. We all live with and cannot escape from uncertainties, difficulties, illness, aging, death, and an inability to fully control life events.

Though it's always been this way, our modern times are laden with new threats, such as nuclear warfare, terrorism, global warming, and other environmental catastrophes in the making, as well as a growing sense of alienation and disconnection. We often don't feel comfortable within ourselves or don't know how to connect with one another, and we often feel estranged or isolated from the natural world.

In recent years, technology and a tsunami of information have accelerated the pace of living, and the complexity of everyday life seems to be mounting. We now have the option of communicating with cell phones, email, instant messaging, text messaging, and social networking sites, making us all available 24/7 to a mad rush of daily activities and demands. We also face an onslaught of news, often piped through these gadgets, with an imbalanced focus on trauma and gloom, overexposing us to worry about world events, health care costs, the obesity epidemic, sleep-deprivation, economic crises, environmental degradation, and so much more.

The fact is, our brains get overwhelmed by this pace of life and bombardment of information, leaving us susceptible to frustration, worry, panic, and even self-judgment and impatience. Given this context, it isn't surprising that many people become so worried or depressed that they demand or are given medications to help balance them out. While taking medications can sometimes be essential for health and well-being, it's also important to cultivate inner resources for dealing with stress, pain, and illness.

Our improvements in technology have brought advancements that border on the miraculous, and at the same time, many of us no longer even know our neighbors. We purchase more and more things yet often feel like we don't have enough. Our educational systems and society teach us facts and information but often don't teach us how to live, and value, a life of integrity. This has left many of us feeling separated, disconnected, and unsafe.

In fact, stress and anxiety have risen to a point where we're beginning to worry about our worrying! The National Institute of Mental Health reported that approximately forty million American adults suffer from anxiety disorders (National Institute of Mental Health 2008). Stress and anxiety affect physical health and have been associated with numerous medical conditions, including cardiovascular disease, cancer, and reproductive disorders. On a societal level, the increasing need for treatment of stress-related problems has led to escalating medical costs, with the result that many people are unable to afford basic health care. And, of course, the various difficulties created by stress can have detrimental effects on quality of life and well-being.

Herbert Benson, MD, a pioneer in the field of mind-body medicine, maintains that many people aren't adequately equipped with coping strategies for dealing with stress (Benson 1976). Approximately five billion doses of tranquilizers are prescribed every year (Powell and Enright 1990), and experts at the American Institute of Stress estimate that the annual cost of stress in the United States—to industries alone—is a monumental figure of approximately $300 billion (American Institute of Stress 2009). Clearly the costs would be much higher if we considered all impacts on individuals and society. This underscores why there's such an urgent need to find alternative ways to cope with stress and anxiety.

In 1979, Jon Kabat-Zinn, Ph.D., a molecular biologist with a long-term meditation practice, founded the Mindfulness-Based Stress Reduction (MBSR) Program at the University of Massachusetts Medical Center. His early research with patients suffering from anxiety and chronic pain showed significant reductions in symptoms (Kabat-Zinn 1982; Kabat-Zinn et al. 1992). Since then, an exponentially increasing amount of research has accumulated on the benefits of mindfulness in dealing with stress, depression, substance abuse, pain, and illness. Recently, this effective approach has finally made the leap into mainstream culture. The numbers speak for themselves: A Google search for "mindfulness" results in millions of hits, and mindfulness-based therapies are growing in popularity, with programs in over 250 hospitals around the country and many more around the globe.

who we are

We want to take a few moments to introduce ourselves. We feel it's important for you to know a bit of our story and how we came to write this book. As you'll discover, both of us came to mindfulness practice out of our own stress and pain, and in search of greater understanding about this wonderful mystery called life. We hope that sharing these stories helps you feel a deeper and more personal connection to us.

Bob Stahl

My spiritual journey began at the age of four, when I had my first realization of death. Over the next few years, I had other powerful experiences that emphasized that death can happen to anyone at any time. By the time I was ten, I had experienced the deaths of three people who were very close to me: my younger brother, Buddy, my best friend, Ellen, and my grandfather, Ben. Impermanence and the fleetingness of life are key concepts in the Buddhist worldview. Most people don't understand these truths deeply until they're adults, perhaps when they or someone they love has a serious illness. It's difficult to learn these frightening truths about the world as a child, when you don't yet have the tools, such as mindfulness, to work with them. Consequently, I grew up pretty confused, filled with grief and fear, and wanting to understand the meaning of life.

In high school I had an important learning experience that pointed me in the right direction to working with fear and mystery. When I was sixteen years old, I drove my parents' 1964 Ford Galaxy around the Boston area in the winter. A few times the car skidded out of control on the snowy roads, and each time I tried desperately to straighten out—but without much success, since I was turning away from the skid. One day I was telling my dad about this, and he said, "Bob, if you really want to get out of a skid, you need to turn *into* it." I thought this was a crazy idea, since it seemed it would only increase the skid, which scared me. So the next time it happened I still tried to steer away from the skid.

The New England winter bore on, and one icy day I took a skid that seemed to be headed for disaster. With nothing left to lose, I turned into the skid, and lo and behold, the car began to straighten out. I felt that a remarkable seed was planted that day and came to see it as a metaphor for life—that if you turn into your fears, you can overcome them. Although it may feel natural to turn away from fear and discomfort, doing so is often fueled by denial, aversion, repression, and suppression—strategies that seldom lead to successful outcomes in the long run.

After graduating from high school I became deeply interested in Eastern philosophy and religion. The *Tao Te Ching* by Lao-tzu (translated by Witter Bynner, 1944) deeply affirmed my inner journey. Reading this small book of eighty-one epigrams was like finding a long-lost friend. I realized that I had been looking for answers about life outside of myself and that they could only be found within me. Epigram 47 (55) had an especially important impact upon me:

> There is no need to run outside
> For better seeing,
> Nor to peer from a window. Rather abide

At the center of your being;
For the more you leave it, the less you learn.
Search your heart and see
If he is wise who takes each turn:
The way to do is to be.

Eventually I moved to San Francisco and enrolled in a masters program in psychology at the California Institute of Integral Studies. That was where I took my first formal mindfulness (vipassana) meditation retreat.

After graduating in 1980, I received an invitation from my first vipassana mindfulness meditation teacher, Dr. Rina Sircar, to go to Burma (now Myanmar) to meet her teacher, the renowned meditation master Taungpulu Sayadaw. In November 1980, I ordained temporarily as a Theravadan Buddhist monk with the name U Candima (Angel of the Moon) in a remote forest monastery in central Burma. During my time there, I had many opportunities to work on my attachments, fears, and pain, instead of trying to escape from them.

In 1981, I disrobed and headed back home to the redwood forests of Northern California to help start the Taungpulu Kaba-Aye Monastery with Dr. Rina Sircar, her students, and the Burmese community. I lived in that monastery for over eight and a half years, studying with my primary meditation teacher, Hlaing Tet Sayadaw. I also went back to school and received a Ph.D. in philosophy and religion, specializing in Buddhism.

In 1989, I left the monastery and married my beloved wife, Jan, and in 1990, an ex-monk friend of mine, Bruce Mitteldorf, sent me a copy of *Full Catastrophe Living*, by Dr. Jon Kabat-Zinn, which describes the mindfulness-based stress reduction program that he developed at the University of Massachusetts Medical Center (Kabat-Zinn 1990). This book revealed what my life's work should be and forever changed my life.

Since 1991, I've taught mindfulness-based stress reduction programs and currently teach at three medical centers. I've worked with thousands of people and many hundreds of health professionals, teaching them mindfulness to help them maximize their lives, even in the midst of pain, stress, and illness. I'm very happy to extend this approach to a wider audience through A *Mindfulness-Based Stress Reduction Workbook*.

Elisha Goldstein

When I was six years old my parents divorced, which left me an angry and confused little boy without the tools to understand and express my hurt and frustration. As I became an adult, I often found myself with some sort of self-help or self-development book in hand, searching for ways to understand my pain.

In my midtwenties, I was living and working in San Francisco in the midst of the Internet boom. While my background was in psychology, I felt drawn to these exciting developments, so I entered the world of sales and management. I soon realized that I was actually quite good at sales, and before long I was getting a lot of attention and recognition. I got caught up in the material world, making money hand over fist, but something always seemed to be missing. I started spending my time living in accordance with the motto "Work hard and play *much* harder." I surrounded myself with people who practiced that same battle cry and avoided those who didn't. I increasingly avoided my family and friends and had to take more days off work because I simply couldn't function with the hangovers. Things seemed out of control and a small part of me was always nagging, "How long do you think you can do this? You're destroying yourself." Whispers about my erratic behavior started circulating among family and friends, and eventually phone calls came pouring in expressing their worry and concern.

I finally realized I was way out of balance and decided to take some time off work to go on a one-month retreat. During my time away, I was able to take a step outside of my madness and become more aware of the destructive habits I had been so blind to. I deeply felt the truth in theologian Abraham Joshua Heschel's saying "Life is routine, and routine is resistance to wonder" (1955, 85). I realized that if I could cultivate a way to break out of my unhealthy routine of avoiding pain and fear, I could come back in touch with the wonder of life and see what life really had to offer. That was the start of a mindfulness practice that has grounded me and helped me reconnect with what matters most to me in life: supporting myself and others to live the lives we want to live.

After returning to San Francisco, I realized I needed to make some changes. I applied to graduate school at the Institute of Transpersonal Psychology, which integrates an East-meets-West philosophy in its curriculum. During that time I also trained as a mindfulness-based stress reduction teacher. I currently run mindfulness-based groups and am in private practice as a clinical psychologist in the West Los Angeles area.

It has been my pleasure to work with Bob Stahl, a highly respected mindfulness teacher, to introduce you to a practice of mindfulness that could very well change your life, as it has mine and tens of thousands of others.

who this workbook is for

This educational and experiential workbook is for anyone living with stress, anxiety, pain, or illness. Weaving mindfulness into your everyday life will not only help reduce stress and anxiety, it will also guide you to a life of greater compassion, health, peace, and well-being.

In addition, this workbook may be helpful for therapists, clinicians, and educators who would like to bring mindfulness to their clients or students as an adjunct to therapy or education. It can also be used in the workplace to help alleviate job stress. You may also want to do this workbook with a group of friends. Mindfulness has become very popular in the worlds of psychology, medicine, neuroscience, education, and business. We hope that this workbook will inspire you to make mindfulness an important part of your life, as a way of being, and believe that as you grow in your own mindfulness practice, you'll be better able to support others on this path.

Although this workbook was inspired by the pioneering mindfulness-based stress reduction programs created by Jon Kabat-Zinn, Ph.D., assisted by Saki Santorelli, Ph.D., at the University of Massachusetts Medical Center, it isn't a substitute for taking the program. (See the Resources section for guidance in finding an MBSR location in your area.) That said, we do believe that this workbook will be an avenue to greater peace and healing in your life.

how to use this workbook

We strongly recommend that you work through this book sequentially, as its organization is based on a well-established and effective program. As you work your way through the book, you'll engage in a variety of mindfulness practices to help reduce the stress and anxiety you feel in response to life's challenges, building your own mindfulness practice along the way. Many of the chapters contain formal mindfulness meditation practices, initially of a fairly short duration and becoming longer as you progress through the book, and all chapters (other than chapter 11) include an informal practice.

Often, change doesn't happen as quickly as we would like. Be assured that change will come with time and practice, and understand that practice is the key to true and lasting change. We suggest that you work with each chapter for at least a week before moving on to the next. This will help integrate the practices into your daily life so that they're more accessible to you, especially when you're dealing with stress or stress-related conditions.

In addition to basic background information, most of the chapters include certain elements to help you gain a greater understanding of mindfulness, develop your own formal and informal practice, schedule your practice, and stay on track with that schedule:

- **Journal.** When each formal practice is first introduced, we include space for you to journal what came up for you. If you like journaling or find that this enhances your practice, consider dedicating a notebook or journal to your mindfulness practice.

- **Mindful exploration.** Throughout the workbook you'll find spaces for mindful self-reflection on various questions to help sustain, deepen, and support your practice.

- **Just do it.** In these text boxes, we offer suggestions on how to bring mindfulness to various day-to-day activities. When you come across one, read it, then put down the book and just do it!

- **FAQ.** Over our many years of teaching mindfulness-based stress reduction, we've found that certain questions come up time and again. These text boxes answer some of the questions we hear most often.

- **Planning your practice.** At the end of every chapter you'll find a checklist reminding you to schedule formal and informal practices over the next week. We recommend using some sort of system or device, such as a daytimer, phone alarm, or electronic calendar.

- **Formal practice logs.** After doing your scheduled formal practices, take the time to use these logs to briefly record what you experienced during each practice.

- **Reviewing your informal practice.** After the formal practice log, we've included a space to review how your informal practices are going. You can use this information to guide you in making any needed adjustments.

At the end of the book, in chapter 11, we'll give you suggestions on how to maintain your mindfulness practice as a way of life. To enhance the effectiveness of your practice and the work you do with this book, we recommend that you connect with a larger community of your peers at www.mbsrwork book.com. There you'll find like-minded people who can support you in the process of cultivating your mindfulness practice. You're likely to find that others appreciate connecting with you for your support, and to share, discuss, and learn more about mindfulness. You'll also find video blogs from both of us and from other meditation teachers.

FAQ

What's the difference between mindfulness meditation and other forms of meditation?

There are essentially two forms of meditation: insight and concentration. Mindfulness is considered insight meditation since it brings full attention to the body and mind in the present moment without trying to alter or manipulate the experience. Whatever is occurring in the body (sights, sounds, smells, tastes, sensations) or mind, the task is simply to observe its ever-changing nature. With the practice of mindfulness, you begin to discover the causes of your own suffering and find a pathway to greater freedom. In concentration meditation, on the other hand, the focus is on concepts, imagery, or a mantra. A sense of tranquility is one of the benefits of the mind becoming deeply absorbed with the meditation object in a one-pointed way. The distinguishing difference is that with concentration meditation, you become one with the object of focus, leading to greater meditative absorption, whereas with insight meditation you begin to see the ever-changing nature of body and mind and the difficulties that are generated from grasping, aversion, and the self-limiting definitions of who you think you are. These insights deepen your understanding of what fuels your stress and suffering and lead to greater balance and peace.

meditation practice suggestions

Here are some suggestions to help you prepare for and develop your practice. We recommend that you use the audio CD included with this book as you learn each new practice. It includes twenty-one different mindfulness meditation practices that add up to over eight and a half hours. The tracks are in MP3 format, which can be played on a computer, MP3 player, or MP3 CD player. Listening to the CD will allow you to deepen your practice, since you won't have to read and refer back to the book as you're practicing. Continue using the CD until you're thoroughly familiar with each practice—or longer if you like. Another advantage to using the CDs is that it paces the practice for you. If you must practice without the CD or choose to, simply set a timer for the length of the practice. For longer practices done without the CD, you'll need to pause longer after each paragraph of text.

As you go through the book, we offer a suggested schedule for practice to help you establish a good foundation. Do the best you can to stick to this schedule. As you move through the book, you'll learn more practices and have greater flexibility in choosing the practices that work best for you. In chapters 1, 2, and 3, you'll learn a mindful eating practice, a three-minute mindful check-in practice, and a five-minute mindful breathing practice. You'll find lengthier and more in-depth meditations in chapters 4 through 8, some with options for practicing for fifteen, thirty, or forty-five minutes, depending on your schedule or preference. In chapters 9 and 10, on mindfulness in relationships and mindfulness for well-being, we'll offer more informal practices to help you extend mindfulness to these aspects of life as you continue with the formal practices you learned earlier in the book.

Read through the first three chapters within a couple of weeks. With the introductory practices in chapters 1 through 3, it's fine to experiment and vary the way you practice them. For example, after practicing the mindful check-in once a day for a week, the second week you could practice the mindful check-in a few times a day or alternate it with the five-minute breathing practice. You could also combine them into one practice, beginning with the mindful check-in for a few minutes and then adding the breathing practice. The main point is to practice regularly and make the practice your own. Later, when we introduce you to longer meditations in chapters 4 through 8, we highly recommend that you work with each of them for a week.

If at any point you notice that you haven't practiced for days, don't be hard on yourself. Just let it be and notice that you are present once again and can make a plan to practice that day. Ultimately of course, it's up to you to work with the practices in a way that feels right for you.

---

explore: Why Did You Purchase This Workbook?

This is the first of many mindful explorations in this workbook. In these exercises, we pose various questions and invite you to sit, reflect, and then write about whatever arises for you in the present moment. As you write, there is no need to analyze, judge, or figure anything out. Simply write about whatever thoughts, feelings, or bodily sensations you experience in the moment in response to this exploration.

While working with the explorations, we suggest moving through the questions slightly slower than you might normally. There's no need to hurry through this. Take your time and feel into your life, and know that doing these explorations is an incredible gift to yourself. You can write brief answers if you like or, to deepen your experience, try writing longer, without stopping, and see what surfaces. Write to your heart's content, knowing that whatever amount of time you spend with this is right for you. If you need more space, you can write on a separate page or in a mindfulness journal.

What has been going on in your life that led you to purchase this workbook?

_____

_____

_____

_____

_____

_____

_____

What are you hoping to change in your life as you work through this book?

_____

_____

_____

_____

_____

_____

What are some positive things you can say about yourself? Whenever you feel you can't think of anything more, squeeze out something else. Feel free to come back to this page later to write down additional positive things about yourself as you think of them.

_____

_____

_____

_____

_____

_____

_____

Through the years, we've witnessed thousands of people answering these questions as they begin their journey of mindfulness. Some come to our classes because their level of stress is so overwhelming. Others face enormous challenges balancing work and personal life. People come because they're angry, sad, scared, or confused, and others because they're living with pain or illness. All come with the hope for more balance—a way to ease stress and to experience more peace. Many of us get so bogged down or beat down by life that we forget what's positive about ourselves and need to be reminded: "Oh yeah, I am a good person. I do act with kindness toward others. I like my sense of humor. I am a good parent, sibling, or friend."

Before you read on, take a moment to compassionately reflect on, acknowledge, and integrate everything you wrote in this exploration.

How Stressed Are You?

Before you turn to chapter 1, take a moment to explore the stressors in your life. This informal assessment isn't meant to replace a clinical assessment; it's simply intended to help you determine what the current stressors are in your life so you can begin to work with them. There are two steps to this process:

1.   Using the form on the next page, list up to ten situations that you perceive to be current stressors in your life. (We've included extra spaces in case other stressors arise later in your life while you work with this book.) In step 2, you'll rate these situations on a scale of 1 to 10, with 1 being not very stressful and 10 being extremely stressful. For this first step, just be sure to include a range of situations from mildly stressful (rated 2 to 4) to extremely stressful (rated 8 to 10). Although it's fine to be general, listing things like work, school, spouse, traffic, crowds, news, being alone, finances, physical pain, unhealthy eating, poor sleep, and so on, we recommend being more specific. That will give you something more definite to track as you determine whether the situation or your stress level has changed later on. For example, instead of "work," you might say, "When my boss asks me to do the quarterly reports," or instead of "crowds," you might say, "When I go to the grocery store in the evening."

2.   In the column immediately to the right of each stressor, rate each on the scale of 1 to 10 described above, with 1 being not very stressful and 10 being extremely stressful. Leave the rightmost two columns blank. Midway through the book and then again at the end, we'll ask you to come back to this page and rate these same stressors again as a way of monitoring whether there have been any changes in your perceived stress level in response to them.

Here's an example: Sarah, who was involved in an MBSR program, felt a high degree of stress every time her boss asked her to do quarterly reports. She rated it a 7, indicating fairly high stress. When she was halfway through the program, she rated her perceived stress about this again. Through her work with mindfulness, she felt better able to handle the challenge at work, but still felt moderately stressed about it, so she rated it a 5. Toward the end of the program she rated her degree of stress about the same issue once again, and though she still noticed some stress, it was minimal, so she rated it a 2.

One important note: If you rate most of the stressors you list as extremely stressful (8 to 10), you may want to use this book in conjunction with a health care or mental health professional.

Situation	Rating (1-10)		
	Start	Midway	End
When my boss asks me to do quarterly reports	7	5	2

No doubt the stressors you listed on the previous page are the very things that led you to purchase this workbook. Know that the practices you'll learn here have been a great gift to many people in dealing with stress, pain, and illness. Often we discover our greatest strengths while working with these difficulties in life.

---

summary

As you move through this workbook, try to engage in the readings, explorations, and practices in the timelines indicated, and connect with others who are doing the same at www.mbsrworkbook.com. May you deeply know that the time you set aside to engage with this book is a wonderful gift to yourself. As the old saying goes, "A journey of a thousand miles begins with a single step." Congratulations on having taken that first step, and welcome to your journey of mindful living.

As you embark upon this sojourn, may these words from a visionary seventeenth-century poet inspire you to continue meeting the most amazing person you'll ever encounter—yourself:

> Direct your eye-sight inward, and you'le find
> A thousand regions in your mind
> Yet undiscover'd. Travell them, and be
> Expert in home Cosmographie.

—William Habington, "To My Honoured Friend Sir Ed. P. Knight" (1634 [1895], 93)

❋ chapter 1 ❋

what is mindfulness?

Mindfulness is about being fully aware of whatever is happening in the present moment, without filters or the lens of judgment. It can be brought to any situation. Put simply, mindfulness consists of cultivating awareness of the mind and body and living in the here and now. While mindfulness as a practice is historically rooted in ancient Buddhist meditative disciplines, it's also a universal practice that anyone can benefit from. And indeed, being present and mindful is an important concept in many spiritual traditions, including Buddhism, Christianity, Hinduism, Islam, Judaism, and Taoism. In Sanskrit, it's known as *smrti*, from the root word *smr*, meaning "to remember," and in Pali, the language of the earliest Buddhist scriptures, it's known as *sati* (mindfulness).

Today, mindfulness has expanded beyond its spiritual roots and even beyond psychology and mental and emotional well-being. Physicians are prescribing training in mindfulness practice to help people deal with stress, pain, and illness. Mindfulness has entered the mainstream in the West and is exerting an influence in a wide variety of contexts, including medicine, neuroscience, psychology, education, and business. As an indicator of its popularization, it has even made an appearance in the blockbuster film *Star Wars*, with just one example being Jedi Master Qui-Gon Jinn telling the novice Obi-Wan Kenobi, "Be mindful!"

In the words of Walpola Rahula, author of the Buddhist classic *What the Buddha Taught*, "[Mindfulness] is simply observing, watching, examining. You are not a judge but a scientist" (1974, 73). You can certainly apply this approach to sensory information and the world around you, and in this book we'll guide you in practices that do just that. However, some of the greatest benefits of mindfulness come from examining your mental processes in this way, observing them dispassionately, as a scientist would. Because this allows great insight into habitual ways of thinking, it has a profound power to alleviate stress and suffering.

After beginning her mindfulness practice, a psychologist friend once remarked that observing her mind revealed it had two modes of operation: either rehearsing or rehashing her life. Before she began observing her thoughts, she hadn't realized how busy her mind was and how often she wasn't present for what was happening in the moment. She said, "Can you imagine if we could bottle all the rehearsing and rehashing we do? We wouldn't have an energy crisis." We've told this story often in our mindfulness classes, and many people nod, laugh, and acknowledge their own compulsion to rehearse and rehash. Yet the present moment is the only place where life may be fully lived. Herein lies one of the greatest benefits of mindfulness: helping us live in the here and now—and helping us become more aware of ourselves.

It is stunning to read these words of St. Augustine written over 1,600 years ago: "Men go forth to marvel at the heights of mountains and the huge waves of the sea, the broad flow of the rivers, the vastness of the ocean, the orbits of the stars, and yet they neglect to marvel at themselves" (2002, 180). While many things have changed since St. Augustine's time, clearly some things haven't. How can it be that all of these centuries later, we still so seldom marvel at ourselves? This is a poignant reminder that it's part of the human condition to tend to lose touch with the wonder or mysteries of life.

An all too common example in Western culture is getting so caught up in the material world that we forget about love, compassion, and generosity. The antidote is mindfulness: a simple and direct practice of moment-to-moment observation of the mind-body process through calm and focused awareness without judgment. As you come to see life as a process of constant change, you can begin to acknowledge all aspects of experience—pleasure and pain, fear and joy—with less stress and more balance.

Because mindfulness can serve as a powerful vehicle for greater understanding of the psyche and the causes of suffering, it's an effective path to ending suffering. The ancient Buddhist text the Dhammapada says, "Mind is the forerunner of all…conditions. Mind is chief; and they are mind-made" (Thera 2004, 1). This profound statement makes it obvious that paying attention to, or being mindful of, your own mind is of paramount importance. It is said that *intention* is the crux of all actions—that our intentions shape our thoughts, words, and deeds. If the intentions are wholesome, the results will be fruitful and skillful. Conversely, if the intentions are unwholesome, the results will be unfruitful and unskillful. In this way, our minds, through our intentions and thoughts, are the creators of our own happiness and unhappiness.

Read over the following progression a couple of times and take a moment to reflect on it:

1. Intention shapes our thoughts and words.

2. Thoughts and words mold our actions.

3. Thoughts, words, and actions shape our behaviors.

4. Behaviors sculpt our bodily expressions.

5. Bodily expressions fashion our character.

6. Our character hardens into what we look like.

You may be familiar with this line of thinking in the form of the saying that by the time people turn fifty, they get the face they deserve. In either case, this is an interesting insight into one of the many ways the mind directly affects the body.

mindfulness and well-being

By helping you begin to recognize your habitual thinking patterns and other ingrained behaviors, mindfulness can play a significant role in enhancing your psychological and physical well-being. However, it can be difficult to sit back and watch your neuroses and problematic behaviors, as what we discover typically doesn't fit the pretty picture of how we want to see ourselves. In meditation circles, it's said that Tibetan meditation master Chögyam Trungpa once likened this process to having brain surgery without anesthesia, or to having to hear one insult after another.

It can be quite challenging to remain an impartial observer when you sit in a hall of mirrors, face-to-face with your fear, shame, guilt, and other unwelcome but familiar internal visitors. Mindfulness offers a space to step outside of this parade of mental wounds, aversions, and fantasies and simply observe them as they come and go. With time, you can learn to acknowledge difficult feelings and thoughts, see their origins more clearly, and experience deeper states of acceptance and peace.

Although this work is difficult, the journey of discovering your own heart is a noble path. There may come a time when you realize, "What else is there to do?" As Vietnamese Buddhist monk and tireless peace activist Thich Nhat Hanh says, "Every mindful step we make and every mindful breath we take will establish peace in the present moment and prevent war in the future. If we transform our individual consciousness, we begin the process of changing the collective consciousness" (2003, 56). How can you ever bring peace to the world if you don't begin with yourself?

everyday mindfulness

Mindfulness is a way of learning how to relate directly to your life. Because it's about your life, no one else can do it for you or tell you exactly how to do it. Fortunately, it isn't something you have to get or acquire. You already have it within you, it's simply a matter of being present. In fact, in the very moment you recognize you aren't present, you've become present. The moment you see that you've been trapped by your thoughts, you gain the freedom to step out of the trap.

Mindfulness is a way of life that can be practiced in two ways: formally and informally. Formal practice means taking time out each day to intentionally sit, stand, or lie down and focus on the breath, bodily sensations, sounds, other senses, or thoughts and emotions. Informal practice involves bringing mindful awareness to daily activities, such as eating, exercising, chores, relating to others, and basically any action, whether at work, at home, or anywhere else you find yourself.

In Alcoholics Anonymous and other 12-step programs, there's a saying "Take one day at a time." Mindfulness goes further, inviting you to take one moment at a time. Since we really live only in the present moment, why not be there for each moment? You can miss so much if you're consumed with anticipation of the future or rumination about the past. And as you become more mindful of your inner state—your thoughts, emotions, sensations, and mental processes—you'll start to sleep better, be more able to cope with stressful situations, improve your self-esteem, renew your enthusiasm for life and work, and generally just feel better.

Just Do It!

An ounce of practice is better than a ton of theories, so why not do some practice? Pick some task that you normally do on a daily basis, like brushing your teeth or washing the dishes, and try to keep your attention on the task as you do it, bringing all of your senses to the experience. If you're brushing your teeth, remind yourself that you're brushing your teeth, feel and listen to the bristles of the toothbrush against your teeth and gums, and smell and taste the toothpaste in your mouth. If you're washing the dishes, know that you're washing the dishes and take in the feel and sound of the water, the smell of the soap, and visual details you might normally gloss over, such as the iridescence of the bubbles. Try it out and see what you notice.

formal practice: Mindfully Eating a Raisin

At the beginning of most mindfulness-based stress reduction classes, we introduce this practice, which involves eating a raisin mindfully, to demystify the concept of meditation. (If you don't have a raisin, any food will do.)

As you do this practice, put aside all distractions, turn off the phone, and focus direct, clear awareness on each aspect and each moment of the experience. You can practice by listening to track 1 on the enclosed CD or by reading the following text, taking some time with each instruction. If you are reading this meditation, take five minutes or so to do this practice.

Place a few raisins in your hand. If you don't have raisins, any food will do. Imagine that you have just come to Earth from a distant planet without such food.

Now, with this food in hand, you can begin to explore it with all of your senses.

Focus on one of the objects as if you've never seen anything like it before. Focus on seeing this object. Scan it, exploring every part of it, as if you've never seen such a thing before. Turn it around with your fingers and notice what color it is.

Notice the folds and where the surface reflects light or becomes darker.

Next, explore the texture, feeling any softness, hardness, coarseness, or smoothness.

While you're doing this, if thoughts arise such as "Why am I doing this weird exercise?" "How will this ever help me?" or "I hate these objects," then just see if you can acknowledge these thoughts, let them be, and then bring your awareness back to the object.

Take the object beneath your nose and carefully notice the smell of it.

Bring the object to one ear, squeeze it, roll it around, and hear if there is any sound coming from it.

Begin to slowly take the object to your mouth, noticing how the arm knows exactly where to go and perhaps becoming aware of your mouth watering.

Gently place the object in your mouth, on your tongue, without biting it. Simply explore the sensations of this object in your mouth.

When you're ready, intentionally bite down on the object, maybe noticing how it automatically goes to one side of the mouth versus the other. Also notice the tastes it releases.

Slowly chew this object. Be aware of the saliva in your mouth and how the object changes in consistency as you chew.

When you feel ready to swallow, consciously notice the intention to swallow, then see if you can notice the sensations of swallowing the raisin, sensing it moving down to your throat and into your esophagus on its way to your stomach.

Take a moment to congratulate yourself for taking this time to experience mindful eating.

Mindful Eating Journal

What did you notice with the raisin (or whatever food) in terms of sight, touch, sound, smell, and taste? Was anything surprising? Did any thoughts or memories pop up while doing this practice? Take a few moments to write down your reflections.

_____

_____

_____

_____

_____

_____

_____

_____

_____

informal practice: Mindful Eating

Eating is a great focus for mindfulness. After all, everyone has to eat, yet we often do so while distracted by something else, like reading, working, or watching television. As a result, people often don't really taste or even notice what they're eating.

You can extend the approach in the formal practice of eating a raisin to any eating experience, allowing you to practice informally anytime you like. Simply give the experience of eating your full, undivided attention and intentionally slow the process down. Try to be like a scientific researcher, observing the mind and body with curiosity and objectivity, and without judgment. Go ahead and practice this several times over the next week. You're likely to find that you enjoy eating more, while perhaps eating less, as you tune in to what your body really wants and needs.

Elisha's Story: Mindful Eating

Back in my midtwenties, when my life felt out of control, I went on a one-month retreat. Each time we sat down to eat we were instructed to be aware of what we were eating, where it came from, and the people who prepared it and to be thankful for it and eat it mindfully. Since I was resistant to being there in the first place, I dug in my heels on this issue and just continued eating as I always had. Often my mind would be swimming with doubts, questioning my decision to even come to this place, thinking I had more important things to be doing, and worrying about whether I really fit in. Most of the time I would be halfway through the meal before I even really tasted the food.

One day, as another participant in the program was talking to me about the importance of being intentional and present in all the activities we do, I immediately thought of the eating and asked him, "Doesn't it annoy you that they make such a big deal about eating here?" He gently smiled at me, brought out an orange from his knapsack, and said, "Treat this as an experiment. Take this orange and really think about where it came from, how it started from a seed in the ground, how real people cared for the tree to make it healthy and then plucked the fruit from that tree. Think about how this orange was carried from there by many different people before it came to me, and now I'm giving it to you. Now, take this orange and drink it in with all of your senses before even peeling it, much less tasting it. When you are ready to take a bite, chew it slightly slower than you normally would, and then come back to me and let me know how it was for you." And then he left me.

As I sat alone, I noticed some resistance arising but decided to try his experiment. I reflected on all the effort it took for this little orange to get to me, including the fact that it was a gift from him, and noticed that I felt a twinge of appreciation and a smile came to my face. I had to admit I liked that. I looked a little closer and noticed all the tiny indents in the skin. As I slowly peeled the orange, I noticed a mist of citrus spring into the air, as though the orange was rejoicing to be opened, which made me laugh, and then I smelled the pungent aroma. I noticed the contrast between the vivid orange of the outside of the peel and the pale, whitish inside surface. Once the orange was peeled, I brought it closer to my eyes and saw the smooth, veined texture of the outer membrane. As I broke apart one section, I really looked at all of the tiny individual pieces of pulp, swollen with juice. When I finally put a piece of orange on my tongue, tingling sensations ran up my cheeks. All of my attention was on the taste of the orange, and as I began to chew, I felt a rush of sheer delight at the amazing taste of this orange. I had eaten many oranges in my life, but I had never tasted an orange in this way. And then I noticed that the distress I had been feeling was gone, and that I felt calm and at ease.

formal practice: Mindful Check-In

Now we'll introduce to you a brief, three-minute practice to give you another taste of mindfulness: the mindful check-in. This short, powerful practice allows you to recognize how you're feeling physically, mentally, and emotionally and will help you recenter yourself in the present moment. We recommend that you incorporate this practice into your daily life, using it as often as you like during the day and then combining it with the breathing practice you'll learn in chapter 3.

Do this practice in a relaxing environment without distractions, such as the phone. You can do it either lying down or sitting up, but if you lie down and find yourself falling asleep, try a more upright posture. We suggest practicing with your eyes closed, since the main point of focus is your inner experience of your mind and body; however, you may keep them partially open if you prefer. Bring your full, undivided attention to this practice as you listen to track 2 on the enclosed CD or read the text, pausing after each paragraph. If you are reading this meditation, take three minutes or so to do this practice.

Take a few moments to be still. Congratulate yourself for taking this time for meditation practice.

Begin this mindful check-in by feeling into your body and mind and simply allowing any waves of thought, emotion, or physical sensation to just be.

Perhaps this is the first break you've taken amidst a busy day. As you begin to enter the world of being rather than doing, you may notice the trajectory of the feelings that you've been carrying within yourself.

There is no need to judge, analyze, or figure things out. Just allow yourself to be in the here and now, amidst everything that is present in this moment. Spend about three minutes simply checking in with yourself in this way.

As you come to the end of this mindful check-in, again congratulate yourself for doing this practice and directly contributing to your health and well-being.

Mindful Check-In Journal

As soon as you finish your first practice of the mindful check-in, take a moment to write about any thoughts, feelings, and sensations you noticed while doing it.

_____

_____

_____

_____

_____

_____

_____

_____

_____

_____

_____

FAQ

Do I have to sit to meditate?

In many pictures of people meditating, they're sitting in intimidating postures with their eyes closed, which can make the practice seem inaccessible or foreign to beginners. Let us clarify right now that there's no need to assume specific or unusual positions when you meditate. The only instructions are to assume a position where you can remain alert, attentive, and comfortable. It is also helpful to have your spine straight yet not too rigid or lax. Mindfulness isn't about attaining a certain sitting posture or even a certain mental state; it's about waking up to the moment in whatever position you are in—physically and mentally.

a word about schedule and review

Below, and at the end of each chapter, you'll find a checklist entitled Planning Your Practice, which reminds you to do two important steps to support you in applying mindfulness to your daily life. The first step involves creating a schedule for your mindfulness practice and following through on your commitment to this schedule. You're probably familiar with the saying "Old habits die hard." It can be quite easy to just get caught up in your daily routines and not follow through on your practice. Schedule your formal practice in whatever calendar you use for your daily life and try to observe this special time with the same discipline as you would a doctor's appointment. After all, it's something you're doing for your well-being, and it can help improve your mental and physical health.

The second step involves reviewing your practice to see how it went. When people begin a new practice, they're often dedicated and enthusiastic at first, and then it begins to fade away. Day-to-day tasks can get in the way, and unexpected demands and obstacles may arise. It's important to set aside some time to reflect on what's working and what isn't so you can adjust your practice as needed. For example, you may notice that you're able to practice in the morning more often than the evening, or that you're more likely to be interrupted at certain times. You might notice that you weren't able to do a certain practice one week, but you were successful the next week. What was the difference? The purpose of this review isn't to judge your efforts as good or bad, but to create awareness around what works and what doesn't work for you and how you can remain effective in your practice. Schedule the review to occur about one week after you've begun each practice.

❧ *Planning and Reviewing Your Practice* ❧

In later chapters, you'll have a wider variety of formal practices to choose from. For now, schedule the formal practice from this chapter on your calendar over the next week. Try to practice at least five days a week. Also schedule a time about a week from now when you'll review your practice to see how it's going.

Formal Practice

☐ Mindful Check-In

Again, you'll have a wider variety of informal practices to choose from as you work forward in this book. For now, start to integrate the informal practice from this chapter into your daily life.

Informal Practice

☐ Mindful Eating

Formal Practice Log

Each time you do a formal practice, fill out the following log. As you fill it out, and as you look back over the previous week's practice, think about how your practice has been going. Do you notice any patterns about what works best for you? What changes could you make to sustain the discipline? In case you're unsure of how to use the log, we've provided an example.

Date and Formal Practice	Time	Thoughts, feelings, and sensations that arose during this practice and how you felt afterward
12/21 Mindful check-in	8 a.m.	My mind kept wandering to all the work I had to do today. I noticed a tightening in my chest at times, but it subsided. That tightness in my chest was anxiousness, and I felt more calm after the practice.

Reflecting on Informal Practice

Take some time every day to reflect on at least one instance of informal practice. You can use what you learn from these reflections to deepen your daily informal practice. Again, we've included an example to help you see how to use the log.

Practice	What was the situation?	What did you notice before?	What did you notice after?	What did you learn?						
Mindful eating	I was having lunch with a friend and noticed I was almost finished eating but hadn't really tasted the food.	Emotions: Anxiousness. Thoughts: "Boy do I have a lot of work left to do at the office." Sensations: Tension in shoulders.	When I brought my attention to the taste of the food and the sensations of chewing, my body began to calm and I noticed how wonderful the food tasted. I felt less frazzled and enjoyed my meal a lot more.	When I slow down in my eating, I notice that I taste the food more, and that this can be like an island of calm in a busy day. I also learned how much I like beets in my salad!						

mindfulness and the mind-body connection

The substantial and significant link between mindfulness and stress reduction is centered within the mind-body connection. Although Western medicine has tended to view the mind-body connection as pseudoscience or a fringe concept, this attitude is changing as neuroscientists discover and chart the neural pathways that connect thoughts and emotions to physiology. This exciting field of science has established that thoughts and emotions are indeed interconnected with the physical process of the body.

When you experience stress, the body produces hormones such as cortisol and neurotransmitters such as epinephrine and norepinephrine. Physiological responses to stress have been crafted by our evolution as a species. In prehistoric times, when a person encountered a life-threatening situation such as being attacked by an animal, the body needed to handle the emergency immediately. To do so, the body's physical energy is redirected in ways that help us fight, flee, or freeze in response to any danger, which is why this reaction has come to be known as the fight, flight, or freeze response.

Life is different now, and while most of us seldom face immediate, life-threatening dangers such as an attacking animal, we do face a multitude of daily stressors, and the body doesn't always know the difference. As a result, the fight, flight, or freeze response can arise due to being stuck in traffic, feeling overwhelmed at work, or worrying about finances or health. How we respond has less to do with the actual event than how we make meaning of the event (Siegel 2001). If your brain perceives danger even when there isn't an imminent physical threat and this automatic reaction occurs repeatedly and remains unchecked, your level of stress can build over time. When cortisol and the neurotransmitters epinephrine and norepinephrine continue to surge through your body, you can go into a kind of hyperadrenaline overdrive. Your health will suffer, as this condition takes energy away from the immune system and other important physiological systems, leaving them less able to perform their functions.

the autonomic nervous system

To understand how stress harms the body, it's helpful to become familiar with the autonomic nervous system. This part of the nervous system works at an involuntary level to regulate vital bodily functions, including the brain, heart, respiration, and many functions of the internal organs and glands. It's comprised of two neural pathways: the sympathetic nervous system and the parasympathetic nervous systems. These pathways have opposing functions that are complementary and serve to balance each other. You can think of the sympathetic system as an accelerator and the parasympathetic system as a brake.

The brain seems to constantly be evaluating whether situations are safe or not. When it detects a potential threat, it has three options: fight, flee, or freeze. When the brain thinks it can take action against the threat, whether by fighting or by fleeing, the sympathetic nervous system kicks in, creating many physiological changes to support heightened activity, such as shallow breathing, increased heart rate and blood pressure, and the release of endorphins to numb pain. Simultaneously, less crucial functions, such as the immune, digestive, and reproductive systems, slow down or temporarily come to a halt. This response can enable a firefighter to carry a three-hundred-pound man down twenty flights of stairs or help you run faster and farther than you normally could. On the other hand, if the brain thinks the situation is hopeless and no action will help, it opts for the freeze response, activating the parasympathetic nervous system, which lowers blood pressure and heart rate, which can aid in immobilizing the body and storing energy. In extreme situations, this can cause fainting.

Once the brain decides that you're out of danger, it activates systems that rebalance the body. In a personal communication, psychiatrist Daniel Siegel, codirector of the UCLA Mindful Awareness Research Center and author of *The Mindful Brain*, said, "The key to a mindful approach to stress involves activating a self-engagement system that likely involves attuning to the self and creating an inner sense of love without fear, which may be at the heart of the relaxation state."

In neuroscience, emotions and thoughts are viewed as being comprised of chemicals and electrical impulses that affect multiple physiological systems, including immunity, the musculoskeletal system, digestion, circulation, and respiration, and as a result, emotions and thoughts can be contributing factors in both health and illness. And because the brain doesn't distinguish between psychological and physiological danger, activating the same physiological responses in either case (Siegel 2001), something as simple and innocuous as waiting in line or dealing with traffic can set off the stress reaction. When day-to-day stress is prolonged and seldom subsides, your body doesn't get a chance to rebalance itself, and the effects can be disastrous, contributing to a long list of ailments, including high blood pressure, muscle tension, skin problems, anxiety, insomnia, gastrointestinal and digestive complaints, and a suppressed immune system, which compromises your ability to fight disease.

stress reaction and stress response

What if you could become mindful of your stress reactions and learn to respond to them in a more constructive and harmonious way? When you become aware of the stress in your life and how it affects your body and mind, you can begin to develop skills to bring greater balance to your life and how you respond to stress. In *Full Catastrophe Living* (1990), Jon Kabat-Zinn makes an important distinction between a stress reaction and a stress response. *Stress reactions* are generally fueled by unconscious habitual patterns, often learned from past challenges and experiences. These patterns include maladaptive coping techniques such as smoking, substance abuse, workaholism, and general busyness and in the long run often lead to mental and physical breakdown. A *stress response*, on the other hand, involves acknowledging emotions rather than suppressing them while also developing tools for working with them. As you learn to respond to stress mindfully, you can gradually begin to break the old default patterns of unawareness associated with stress reactions, opening the door to new ways of working with stress and transforming it. Awareness is like bringing a light to the darkness of mindless reactions. Once you can see them more clearly, you can choose to respond more skillfully.

One of the many benefits of mindfulness is that it allows you to be with a wide range of experiences, including difficult internal states such as agitation and fear. Because it brings clarity and awareness to all internal experiences, it can play a strategic role in balancing the accelerator and brake of the sympathetic and parasympathetic nervous systems. In *The Mindful Brain* (2007), Daniel Siegel describes this stabilization of attention as an even hovering of awareness that allows for the observation of different mind states, including stress reactions. Further, he believes that mindfulness allows the prefrontal cortex of the brain to balance the two branches of the autonomic nervous system in a flexible and adaptive manner, creating greater equanimity. This combination of observation and equanimity can go a long way in helping you avoid getting caught up in your mental content and mindless reactions.

Because of how the mind-body system is so intricately interwoven, this capacity to transform stress and respond with greater equanimity also has profound implications for physical health. The best possible medical care begins with self-care, which allows you to exert some control over your own well-being. Practicing mindfulness is a powerful means of taking an active role in your own self-care and improving your overall wellness.

mindfulness and its pivotal role in stress reduction

Today, there are over 250 mindfulness-based stress reduction programs in major medical centers throughout the United States, as well as programs throughout much of the world. Mindfulness-based approaches have proven effective in decreasing symptoms of anxiety (Miller, Fletcher, and Kabat-Zinn 1995), obsessive-compulsive disorder (Baxter et al. 1992), and chronic pain (Kabat-Zinn, Chapman, and Salmon 1987). They've also been shown to be helpful in reducing the detrimental effects of psoriasis (Kabat-Zinn et al. 1998), increasing a sense of empathy and spirituality (Shapiro, Schwartz, and Bonner 1998), increasing well-being (Brown and Ryan 2003), preventing relapse in depression (Segal et al. 2007) and drug addiction (Parks, Anderson, and Marlatt 2001), and decreasing stress and enhancing quality of life for those struggling with breast and prostate cancer (Carlson, L., et al. 2007).

You might wonder how mindfulness can be so beneficial in regard to so many different difficulties and disorders. The answer lies in its very nature. This practice of moment-to-moment nonjudgmental awareness brings focus to whatever is happening in the moment, and it is only in the present moment that you can make changes. As you open your awareness to what is imbalanced and come to recognize unconscious habitual tendencies, you can begin to make new choices that promote well-being and balance.

Gary Schwartz, a psychologist who studies stress, has developed a model of a health feedback loop in which he attributes the ultimate origin of disease to disconnectedness from thoughts, sensations, and emotions, and the origin of health to connectedness with these internal experiences (Kabat-Zinn 1990). The feedback loop he outlines suggests that if you're unaware of your internal stress reactions and how they express themselves in thoughts, sensations, and emotions, you're disconnected, which can take your body and mind out of balance. Conversely, awareness automatically creates connection, helping you recognize what you're experiencing so that you can do what's necessary to return to balance.

An everyday example of how awareness can decrease stress is the common experience of getting stuck in traffic. Because it's easy to be unaware of the impact stress has on the body and mind, you may not have noticed tension throughout your body, rapid or irregular breathing, or that you're gripping the steering wheel so tightly that your knuckles are turning white. It's even less likely that you'll notice other, more hidden impacts of anxiety and irritation, such as elevated heart rate, blood pressure, or body temperature. However, once you become aware of your physical tension, you've returned to the present moment and can release your death grip on the steering wheel. And once you see that you're breathing rapidly and irregularly, you can stabilize your breath by breathing mindfully, which will gradually regulate other internal symptoms of stress, including heart rate and blood pressure.

Because mindfulness allows you to see your experience clearly, it can help you become more aware of how stress affects you. Then you can choose a more skillful response. In this way, you can become a more active participant in your health and well-being and experience any moment, no matter how difficult or intense, with more balance and peace.

mindfulness and the brain

A number of studies have demonstrated that practicing mindfulness causes healthy changes in the brain, supporting anecdotal evidence from the real-life experiences of thousands of people we personally have worked with, who have enjoyed increased well-being, focus, and peace as a result of their practice.

For example, in 2003, Dr. Richard Davidson, director of the Laboratory for Affective Neuroscience at the University of Wisconsin–Madison, Jon Kabat-Zinn, and colleagues published results of a study that examined the effects of an eight-week MBSR program on the mental and physical health of a group of employees at a biotech company. Of the forty-one people in the study, twenty-five participated in the MBSR program and sixteen didn't. The electrical activity of each participant's brain was measured before and immediately after the program and then four months later. The research found that the meditation group had significant increases in activity in the left side of the brain's frontal area as compared to the control group. This region of the brain is associated with positive affect and emotion regulation. Davidson's research showed that individuals with greater activation in this region recover more quickly following a stressful event compared with individuals with less activation in this region. The 2003 study also revealed interesting links with immune system functioning. At the end of the eight-week program, all participants were given a flu vaccination. Those who meditated had significant increases in antibodies compared to the control group, suggesting that meditation can help boost the immune response.

In 2005, Sara Lazar, Ph.D., an instructor at Harvard Medical School, published research that found a measurable difference in the brains of people who routinely meditate compared to those who don't. Using MRI brain scans, she found thicker regions in the frontal cortex, an area responsible for reasoning and decision making, in those who had a consistent mindfulness practice compared to those who didn't. Additionally, she found a thicker insula, which is involved in sensing internal sensations and thought to be a critical structure in the perception of emotional feelings (Lewis and Todd 2005). She suggested that because the cortex and insula normally start deteriorating after age twenty, mindfulness meditation might help make up for some of the losses due to aging. In a personal communication, she told us that she believes "meditation can have a serious impact on your brain long beyond the time when you're actually sitting and meditating, and this may have a positive impact on your day-to-day living."

Based on a review of current research, along with personal accounts, Dr. Daniel Siegel (2007) suggests that the practice of mindfulness uses the social neural circuitry of the brain to help us become more attuned to ourselves, which results in greater physical, psychological, and social well-being. In essence, when paying attention to our minds, we use the same mechanisms in the brain that we've always used to scan for the feelings, intentions, and attitudes of others (social circuitry). He says that the way we pay attention affects *neural plasticity*—the ability to change our neural connections in response to our experiences. In a statement that might blow your mind, he says, "Here we see the notion that the mind is using the brain to create itself" (2007, 32). Ponder that for a minute or a million. He explains that mindfulness practice can affect the prefrontal area of the brain, which has integrative functions that impact many areas of the brain and body, suggesting that mindfulness has a positive influence on resilience, self-regulation, and well-being.

Mindfulness and brain research is certainly a hot topic these days, and studies are ongoing. For example, the Mind and Life Institute has gathered some of the world's foremost scientists, the Dalai Lama, and other Nobel Prize winners, to collaborate on research with experienced meditators. Other research is being coordinated by the Center for Contemplative Mind in Society, which has recently developed a project to work with Army caregivers. The Center for Contemplative Mind in Society also gathers information on various studies with a bearing on mindfulness and the brain. For example, one recent study (Brefczynski-Lewis et al. 2007) found that in long-term meditators emotional sounds caused less activation of the amygdala, a part of the brain that's associated with processing fear and aggression. This suggests that a long-term meditation practice may be associated with significant decreases in emotionally reactive behavior.

Another recent study (Lutz et al. 2008) found that meditation has a significant effect on regions of the brain involved with empathetic responses. When Buddhist monks practicing compassion meditation were presented with emotional sounds, both happy and distressed, various regions of the brain were activated in a way that suggested enhanced detection of these sounds, along with more mental activity in response to them, in comparison to a group of novice meditators. Moreover, experienced meditators also had a greater response to distressed emotional sounds than novices, and all meditators showed a greater response while meditating than when at rest, indicating that meditation has a direct effect on the mental circuitry involved in empathy.

This is just a small sample of the growing body of research on the psychobiological benefits of meditation. This scientific validation of what so many people have experienced firsthand not only promotes the understanding of the science behind mindfulness, it also opens the door for further research into how we might be able to use mindfulness practices to work with and support many different forms of stress, pain, and illness.

mindfulness and everyday stress

To get a sense of what a huge impact mindfulness can have on your well-being, consider how often minor daily stresses affect your thoughts and emotions, which in turn exert effects on your body. You may feel stressed-out when waiting in a line at the bank or the post office, when driving in traffic or along an unfamiliar route, when facing a deadline, or when having an uncomfortable conversation. You can even experience stress reactions as a result of anticipating or remembering such events. Though these stresses seem fairly minor, they can cause all sorts of symptoms, such as muscular tension, headaches, insomnia, gastrointestinal upset, and skin conditions. Long-term stress can also be a factor in serious diseases such as cancer, heart disease, and dementia, particularly if you rely on unhealthy strategies to cope with stress, such as smoking, substance abuse, overeating, or overworking.

One of the gifts that mindfulness offers is helping you recognize that there are choices in how you respond to any stressful situation. Viktor Frankl, psychiatrist and holocaust survivor, describes this eloquently: "Between stimulus and response there is a space. In that space is our power to choose our response. In our response lies our growth and our freedom" (Pattakos 2008, viii). Even amidst Frankl's imprisonment, he found ways to provide comfort and healing to those around him, underscoring that, with awareness, everyone has freedom of choice how to respond. The key is awareness. Of course, conditioning is a powerful force that can make it difficult to change. Just as water finds the path of least resistance, you'll tend to fall back on habits because in many ways this is the easiest course to follow. This includes habitual ways of seeing and reacting. To help provide motivation for the challenging work of turning off your autopilot and resisting habitual reactions and behaviors, the next exercise will help you explore how stress is impacting your life. Becoming truly aware of the stress in your life and how you interact with it is a necessary first step in choosing new responses that will serve you better.

FAQ

How is meditation different from relaxation?

While meditation can certainly bring on feelings of relaxation, it also may not. Your intention is what makes the difference. When you want to relax, you can engage in a wide variety of activities, from watching TV, reading a book, lying in a hammock, soaking in a bubble bath, doing breathing exercises...the list goes on and on. In mindfulness meditation, the intention is simply to place nonjudgmental attention on whatever object of awareness you've chosen. So if you're practicing mindfulness with eating a raisin, you're tuning in to all of your senses, not for the purpose of relaxation, but for the purpose of truly and deeply experiencing the present moment. Practicing meditation for the purpose of relaxation can actually be a trap; if you meditate and don't feel relaxed, your mind might start racing with thoughts about how it isn't working. This could lead to feelings of frustration, anxiety, and disappointment, which may send you on a downward spiral toward becoming anxious or depressed.

explore: How Is Stress or Anxiety Affecting Your Life?

Take some time to reflect on the following questions, noticing whatever comes up in your thoughts, feelings, and sensations. When you're ready, write some of your thoughts below. You may have more to write for some questions than others; this is fine.

How is stress or anxiety about people affecting your life?

_____

_____

_____

_____

_____

_____

_____

_____

How is stress or anxiety about work affecting your life?

_____

_____

_____

_____

_____

_____

_____

_____

How is stress or anxiety about the world affecting your life?

_____

_____

_____

_____

_____

_____

_____

How is stress or anxiety about food and eating habits affecting your life?

_____

_____

_____

_____

_____

_____

_____

How is stress or anxiety about sleep and sleeplessness affecting your life?

_____

_____

_____

_____

_____

_____

_____

_____

How is stress or anxiety about exercise or lack of physical activity affecting your life?

_____

_____

_____

_____

_____

_____

_____

We want to acknowledge and validate whatever you wrote about how your life is impacted by stress or anxiety about relationships, work, your view of the world, eating habits, sleep, and physical activity. As awareness grows, you can begin to see more clearly how stress and anxiety affects so many areas of your life. While this is normal, the fact that you are now becoming aware of its persuasiveness is an important first step toward greater well-being.

Before you move on, take a moment to compassionately reflect on, acknowledge, and integrate everything you wrote in this exploration.

informal practice: Weaving Mindfulness Throughout Your Day

From the moment you wake up to the moment you lay your head on the pillow at the end of your day, you have the opportunity to engage mindfulness as a way of life. However, if you're like most people, as soon as you awaken, the mind is already busy compiling to-do lists and thinking about how you'll accomplish everything. When you're at work, you may find yourself thinking about your next task rather than what's before you, or just wishing the workday was over. A feeling of being rushed or overwhelmed may follow you into your household tasks, relationships, and even recreation, so that no matter what you're doing, part of your mind is thinking about other things you need to do or rehashing what has occurred.

By choosing to become mindful throughout the day, you can bring greater focus and appreciation to whatever situation you find yourself in. You'll also feel more calm and at peace. As you continue to grow in mindfulness, you'll see the potential for informal practice in any situation. If you need some help getting started, here are some suggestions for informal ways to weave mindfulness into your day:

- As you open your eyes in the morning, instead of jumping out of bed, take a few moments to do a mindful check-in. By starting the day with greater present moment awareness, you'll set the stage for a greater sense of calm and equanimity during challenging moments throughout your day.

- As you bathe, notice if your mind is already thinking, planning, and rehearsing for the day ahead. When you become aware of this, gently bring your mind back to the moment: being in the shower, smelling the soap, feeling the sensation of the water on your body, listening to the sound of it in the shower.

- If you live with others, try taking a few moments to listen and connect with them mindfully before you head out for the day.

- As you approach your car, walk more slowly, check in with your body, and notice any tension. Try to soften it before you begin your drive.

- When you drive, find opportunities to try driving a little slower. Use red lights as a reminder to notice your breathing.

- Walking is something we definitely tend to do on autopilot. As you walk to your office or to run errands, walk differently. For example, you might walk more slowly, or you could breathe in for three steps, then breathe out for three steps. Notice the sensations of walking—in your feet and throughout your body.

- When doing tasks at work, block out time to focus on a group of similar tasks. For example, block out time just for planning and don't attend to other tasks during that time. If you can, turn off your e-mail during times when you're focusing on other tasks.

- If possible, maybe once a week, have a meal by yourself in silence, eating slightly slower than you usually do and really tuning in to flavors and textures as you eat.

- Throughout the day, do mindful check-ins from time to time. You can schedule them on your calendar, or you can link them to certain activities, such as prior to checking your email or before you drive in rush hour traffic.

- It's counterproductive to rush home to relax, so try driving home mindfully and slightly slower. Feel your hands on the steering wheel, and mindfully take in each moment. You could turn off the radio and reflect on what you did that day. What was positive, and what would you like to do better? Another possibility is to intentionally plan how you would like to be when you get home, perhaps putting mindful listening on the agenda.

- When you get home, do a mindful check-in before you walk in the door, noticing if your body is tense. If it is, try to soften those muscles by breathing into them with awareness and just letting them be.

As you begin to integrate informal practice into your daily life, take some time to reflect on your experiences. What did you do? What did you notice about yourself before and after the practice? How did you act or react to others? What are you learning from informal practice? If you like, you can write about this in your journal.

Just Do It!

Take a moment right now to notice the connection between what you're thinking and how you're feeling physically and emotionally. Spend a few moments observing your thoughts, emotions, and physical sensations and considering how they may relate to one another. Then take this practice with you into your daily life. For example, notice your initial reactions when you're stuck in line or in traffic, and how bringing mindfulness to the situation offers you the opportunity to respond differently.

a word on connecting with others

Practicing alone can be difficult. We encourage you to connect with others for support and motivation and to benefit from their insights. If you haven't already spent some time at www.mbsrworkbook.com, go ahead and try it now. See what others are saying about their practice. Sometimes sharing with others and understanding their experience can help you maintain and deepen your practice.

Planning and Reviewing Your Practice

In later chapters, you'll have a wider variety of formal practices to choose from. For now, schedule the formal practice from chapter 1, the mindful check-in, on your calendar over the next week. Try to practice daily or near daily. Also schedule a time about a week from now when you'll review your practice to see how it's going.

Formal Practice

☐   Mindful Check-In

Now you have two informal practices to integrate into your daily life.

Informal Practices

☐   Weaving Mindfulness Throughout Your Day

☐   Mindful Eating

Formal Practice Log

Each time you do a formal practice, fill out the following log. As you fill it out, and as you look back over the previous week's practice, think about how your practice has been going. Do you notice any patterns about what works best for you? What changes could you make to sustain the discipline?

Date and Formal Practice	Time	Thoughts, feelings, and sensations that arose during this practice and how you felt afterward

Reflecting on Informal Practice

Take some time every day to reflect on at least one instance of informal practice. You can use what you learn from these reflections to deepen your daily informal practice.

Practice	What was the situation?	What did you notice before?	What did you notice after?	What did you learn?

how to practice mindfulness meditation

In the previous two chapters, we've introduced you to both formal and informal mindfulness practices. In this chapter, you'll begin to deepen your practice with mindful breathing, a fundamental formal practice. Because your breath is always with you, this is a practice you can take with you anywhere, and something you can integrate with informal practice. As you blend your formal and informal practices and extend them, mindfulness will become a way of life. With time, you'll learn to bring mindfulness to your thoughts, words, and actions, and ultimately into everything you do, so that whatever you experience in life becomes your practice.

In this chapter we'll take a look at the nuts and bolts of developing a formal mindfulness meditation practice, one step at a time. As you move through this process and invest your time in it, know that this is an incredible gift that you're giving yourself. Meditation will help you access deep inner resources for your well-being. In this busy and often stressful world, mindfulness meditation can serve as an oasis, a refuge in the midst of the hustle and bustle where you can come home to your self.

attitudes of mindfulness

The practice of mindfulness is like cultivating a garden: it flourishes when certain conditions are present. In terms of mindfulness, these conditions include the following eight attitudes, which are essential to mindfulness practice:

- **Beginner's mind.** This quality of awareness sees things as new and fresh, as if for the first time, with a sense of curiosity.

- **Nonjudgment.** This quality of awareness involves cultivating impartial observation in regard to any experience—not labeling thoughts, feelings, or sensations as good or bad, right or wrong, fair or unfair, but simply taking note of thoughts, feelings, or sensations in each moment.

- **Acknowledgment.** This quality of awareness validates and acknowledges things as they are.

- **Nonstriving.** With this quality of awareness, there is no grasping, aversion to change, or movement away from whatever arises in the moment; in other words, nonstriving means not trying to get anywhere other than where you are.

- **Equanimity.** This quality of awareness involves balance and fosters wisdom. It allows a deep understanding of the nature of change and allows you to be with change with greater insight and compassion.

- **Letting be.** With this quality of awareness, you can simply let things be as they are, with no need to try to *let go* of whatever is present.

- **Self-reliance.** This quality of awareness helps you see for yourself, from your own experience, what is true or untrue.

- **Self-compassion.** This quality of awareness cultivates love for yourself as you are, without self-blame or criticism.

Holding these qualities in mind—reflecting upon them and cultivating them according to your best understanding—will nourish, support, and strengthen your practice. Developing these qualities is a way of channeling your energies into the process of healing and growth. These attitudes are interdependent; each influences the others, and by cultivating one you enhance them all.

mindful breathing

Mindful breathing often serves as the foundation for meditation practices because your breath is always with you, wherever you are, and it can be used as an anchor to the present moment. In essence, all that's involved is simply being mindful when you breathe in and out. There is no need to analyze, count, visualize, or manipulate the breath in any way. Just breathe normally and naturally and be aware of breathing in and out. There are a few methods you can use to focus on your breath. You can be mindful of your breath in your nose, chest, belly, or even your entire body as it breathes in and out.

For dealing with the challenges of stress and anxiety, we sometimes recommend abdominal breathing—breathing from the belly, rather than only into the chest—as this can be very calming. However, if another location is preferable, please listen to your own wisdom. Generally speaking, abdominal or belly breathing is the way we all naturally breathe, especially when we're lying down. To determine if you're breathing from your abdomen, place your hand on your belly and feel whether it expands as you inhale and contracts as you exhale. If it doesn't, turn your attention to breathing more deeply and feeling your belly expand and contract with your breath.

An important benefit of abdominal or belly breathing is that it helps moderate irregular breathing patterns, which often arise due to stress or irritation. Anxiety can lead to shallow, rapid, or sporadic breathing and even hyperventilation, and a full-blown panic attack can cause increased shortness of breath, thoughts of losing control, and pains in the chest. By bringing the breath back into the belly, you can help the body return to balance. So when anxiety arises, first acknowledge the feeling, then gently bring attention to the abdomen and practice mindful belly breathing.

wandering mind

In practicing mindfulness, the mind will inevitably wander. As you start to look closely at the workings of your own mind, you're likely to see firsthand how often you're lost in thoughts of the future or memories of the past. For example, when showering, you may rarely just experience the shower because you're thinking of other things. You've probably had the experience of driving somewhere and realizing that you hardly remember how you got to your destination. There are so many times during the day when you may not be present to what's happening. How often are you actually in the moment while brushing your teeth, folding the laundry, or washing the dishes?

In the practice of mindfulness meditation, you bring your focus to a particular object of awareness, such as the breath. After a short time of practicing, the mind will wander off. This is normal, especially for a mind not trained in concentration. Your job is not to judge yourself, but simply to patiently notice and acknowledge the mind wandering—letting it be—and then gently bring the focus back to the breath. Most of us do this over and over, again and again. Rather than berating yourself, think of it this way: If you weren't mindful, you wouldn't even know you had wandered off. The fact is, in the moment when you realize you aren't present, you have become present. It's that close. Christian mystic St. Francis de Sales spoke to this dynamic: "If the heart wanders or is distracted, bring it back to the point quite gently... And even if you did nothing during the whole of your hour but bring your heart back..., though it went away every time you brought it back, your hour would be very well employed" (Levey and Levey 2009, 64).

Note that bringing the mind back to the present moment is as much a part of the practice as is concentrating on the primary object. It's important to not repress or suppress thoughts and feelings as they arise in the present moment. You are learning how to be with them as they are, rather than trying to force anything to be a certain way. It's important to first acknowledge without judgment where your mind went, and then gently bring it back to the object of focus.

Bringing the mind back after it has wandered has three main benefits: The first is that it provides training in concentration. When your mind goes off and you bring it back again and again, gradually your concentration grows. The second benefit is that by coming back into the present moment and noticing where you drifted off to, you may discover that you're filled with self-judgment, worry, sadness, anger, or confusion, perhaps signaling that you need to pay closer attention to and deal with certain things in your life. The third benefit is that when you come back from wandering, you may realize you've been worrying or experiencing other distressing emotions. You may then notice that you're also experiencing related physical symptoms, such as a clenched jaw or an upset stomach. By coming back into the present moment you begin to directly see and experience the mind-body connection in how your thoughts and emotions express themselves in your body.

FAQ

I can't find the time to meditate. What can I do?

Many people have this challenge. May you grow to understand that making time to practice meditation is an incredible gift you give yourself. No one else can give you this gift. On a more practical note, just as you schedule appointments with others in your calendar, you can schedule a date with yourself to practice meditation, even if only for five minutes. Perhaps schedule it next to something you already do on a daily basis. If you have an electronic calendar, use a pop-up alert to remind you to practice.

As you continue working with this book, we'll introduce you to longer practices. Although thirty to forty-five minutes of daily formal meditation is optimal for your health and well-being, just a few minutes of mindfulness a day can be beneficial. We include a variety of practices so that you can easily incorporate mindfulness into your day, whether you're sitting, standing, walking, or lying down.

posture and practice

You may wonder how you should position your body for meditation practice, and how to work with sleepiness, which is a common problem in our on-the-go culture. Here are some tried-and-true recommendations:

- You may sit on the floor, on a meditation cushion (*zafu*), or in a chair. You can also sit on a folded towel or blanket or cushions from your couch. You can even stand or lie on your back, but in the latter case it may be important to set the intention to be fully awake and present.

- Most people meditate with their eyes closed, but if you prefer or are more comfortable doing so, you can keep them partially open. If you choose to keep them open, please remember that the focus is on whatever meditation you are practicing.

- You can fold your hands on your lap or place them on your thighs.

- Position yourself so you can remain alert yet comfortable. Just as the strings on an instrument can be wound too tight or too loose, a meditator can sit too rigidly, causing a lot of discomfort. This may result in not sitting for very long. Conversely, a meditator whose posture is too relaxed may end up falling asleep.

- If sleepiness is an issue, you could meditate while standing or keeping your eyes open. Or perhaps the answer is to take a nap—maybe you really need it—and then come back to the practice when you're more rested. Have compassion for yourself and listen deeply to what you need.

formal practice: Five-Minute Mindful Breathing

Now that you're familiar with some of the important foundations of mindfulness meditation, you're ready to start practicing mindful breathing. As we said before, a beautiful old wisdom saying advises, "An ounce of practice is better than tons of theories." Before we begin, we have one final bit of advice: With any of these practices, the deepest healing occurs when you come to terms with the way things are. This might mean simply noticing and acknowledging stress or anxiety rather than falling into old patterns of running away from it. You may discover that by embracing your fear you find your heart.

Do this practice in a relaxing environment without distractions, such as the phone. You can do it either lying down or sitting up, but if you lie down and find yourself falling asleep, try a more upright posture. Bring your full, undivided attention to this practice as you listen to track 3 on the enclosed CD or read the following meditation, pausing after each paragraph. You can practice anytime throughout the day, combining this practice with the mindful check-in if you like.

Take a few moments to be still. Congratulate yourself for taking some time for meditation practice.

Bring your awareness to your breath wherever you feel it most prominently in your body. It may be at the nose, neck, chest, belly, or somewhere else. As you breathe in normally and naturally, be aware of breathing in, and as you breathe out, be aware of breathing out. Simply maintain this awareness of the breath, breathing in and breathing out.

There is no need to visualize, count, or figure out the breath; just be mindful of breathing in and out. Without judgment, just watch the breath ebb and flow like waves in the sea. There's no place to go and nothing else to do, just be in the here and now, noticing the breath—just living life one inhalation and one exhalation at a time.

As you breathe in and out, be mindful of the breath rising on the inhalation and falling on the exhalation. Just riding the waves of the breath, moment by moment, breathing in and breathing out.

From time to time, attention may wander from the breath. When you notice this, simply acknowledge where you went and then gently bring your attention back to the breath.

Breathing normally and naturally, without manipulating the breath in any way, just be aware of the breath as it comes and goes.

As you come to the end of this meditation, congratulate yourself for taking this time to be present, realizing that this is an act of love. May we be at peace. May all beings be at peace.

Five-Minute Mindful Breathing Journal

Take some time to write about whatever came up for you mentally, emotionally, and physically when doing this practice for the first time.

_____

_____

_____

_____

_____

_____

_____

_____

---

informal practice: Bringing the Eight Attitudes of Mindfulness into Your Life

Try bringing the eight attitudes of mindfulness—beginner's mind, nonjudgment, acknowledgment, nonstriving, equanimity, letting be, self-reliance, and self-compassion—to yourself, other people, and the activities you do. For example, if you're cooking, you can practice doing it as if for the first time. Approaching the task with beginner's mind, feel the textures and experience the aromas as you cut onions, carrots, and greens, without any judgments about yourself, the food, or your cooking. Acknowledge your self-reliance—that you can care for yourself and others by cooking this meal. If this is difficult, view it as an opportunity to practice self-compassion and be aware that you're making your best effort; don't get down if anything doesn't go the way you want it to go. If your mind kicks into high gear and tries to rush through the experience of cooking, practice nonstriving, knowing that you've already arrived to the present moment and coming back to the task at hand. Watching and understanding the impermanent nature of this process as it unfolds, and letting it be, is a practice in equanimity. Notice how your body and mind feel when these attitudes are present, and how your mind and body feel when they aren't. Try bringing this practice into other areas of your daily life and see what happens to your relationship with yourself, others, and the world.

Just Do It!

Practice mindfulness with your senses right now. Simply look around the room or out your window and notice what you see with beginner's mind—as if you were seeing your surroundings for the very first time. Listen to any sounds, smell any scents, and taste any flavors still lingering in your mouth; or, if you're hungry, eat something with intention and mindfulness. Feel into your body and acknowledge whatever you're feeling, physically and emotionally. Also bring your awareness to whatever thoughts come into your mind. When you're finished, thank yourself for taking this time to practice mindfulness, and acknowledge what is was like to check in with your senses, thoughts, and emotions.

 ## *Planning and Reviewing Your Practice*

Here are the formal practices you've learned so far. Go ahead and put them on your calendar over the next week. Try to practice daily or near daily. Also schedule a time about a week from now when you'll review your practice to see how it's going.

Formal Practices

☐   Five-Minute Mindful Breathing

☐   Mindful Check-In

Now you have three informal practices to integrate into your daily life.

Informal Practices

☐   Bringing the Eight Attitudes of Mindfulness into Your Life

☐   Weaving Mindfulness Throughout Your Day

☐   Mindful Eating

Formal Practice Log

Each time you do a formal practice, fill out the following log. As you fill it out, and as you look back over the previous week's practice, think about how your practice has been going. Do you notice any patterns about what works best for you? What changes could you make to sustain the discipline?

Date and practice	Time	Thoughts, feelings, and sensations that arose during this practice and how you felt afterward

Reflecting on Informal Practice

As you increasingly make mindfulness a way of life and extend it into your day-to-day activities, it won't be practical to record your reflections on each instance of informal practice. Still, take some time every day to reflect on at least one instance of informal practice. You can use what you learn from these reflections to deepen your daily informal practice.

Practice	What was the situation?	What did you notice before?	What did you notice after?	What did you learn?

how mindfulness works
with stress reduction

Living with stress and anxiety is much more prevalent than you might imagine. Millions of people suffer and live with the challenges of stress every day, whether from day-to-day events, pain or illness, difficult life events, or, perhaps most typically, a combination of factors. Most of us don't want to talk about our stress and anxiety or face these things within ourselves. Actor and filmmaker Woody Allen once said, "I don't mind dying as long as I don't have to be there" (Bastian and Staley 2009, 9). Though said partly in jest, this is typical of our culture and how we so often deny or avoid facing apprehensions and fears.

We all share similar questions about the mysteries of life, such as who we are, where we come from, and where we're going. We wonder about the meaning of life and the reality of death. We face countless fears each day and, at times, problematic phobias. We may have issues with confidence, and we may have anxiety related to relationships, work, the state of the world, food, or sleep, and the list goes on and on. Our relationships can suffer from breakdowns in communication, whether amongst family, friends, acquaintances, work colleagues or others. Work comes with deadlines to meet or other standards to achieve. It's no surprise that we might have anxiety about the world, given that we live amidst war, terrorism, global climate change, overpopulation, famine, the inevitable natural disasters, and so much more. We may even have anxiety about our anxiety!

As much as we may wish to ignore these concerns or pretend they don't exist, the unfortunate truth is that we can't control the world around us, and there will always be situations capable of pro-voking worry, stress, and anxiety. The answer isn't to turn away; it's to turn toward, like turning into the skid. Mindfulness meditation is extremely useful in this regard, helping you get in touch with these concerns and learning to work with them so that they aren't so paralyzing. As hundreds of thousands of mindfulness practitioners have discovered, it is possible to live with stress and also with less suffering and fear. And although you can't always control or eliminate stressors, you can engage with them differently.

The key is mindfully exploring what may be influencing your relationship to the challenges in your life and examining what works and what doesn't work in dealing with them.

explore: What Works and What Doesn't?

Sometimes difficult or distressing events you've experienced in the past can influence your current stress and anxiety. For example, many people have been wounded, physically or emotionally, in childhood. Likewise, many of us have witnessed traumatic events or had experiences like being humiliated at work or not being accepted by friends.

Take a few minutes to reflect on any past challenges that you might currently be carrying around with you. When you're ready, write as briefly or as in depth on this reflection as you like.

_____

_____

_____

_____

_____

_____

As you've journeyed through life, you've found ways to deal with stress, pain, or illness. For example, you might talk with friends, exercise, meditate, eat healthy foods, or watch a funny movie. In addressing your stress, what have you tried that has been helpful for you in the past? Take a few minutes to sit with this question silently, noticing any thoughts, feelings, and sensations. Just let whatever arises be there without judgment. When you're ready, write as briefly or as in depth on this reflection as you like.

_____

_____

_____

_____

_____

Sometimes you may have chosen unhealthy ways to deal with your challenges. Perhaps you overeat, work too much, watch too much TV, spend hours on the Internet or engaged in e-mail, or use drinking, sex, or drugs to excess. These strategies often feel like they help initially, but they don't help in the long run. In dealing with stress or anxiety, what have you tried that ultimately didn't seem to help? Take a few minutes to sit with this question silently, noticing any thoughts, feelings, and sensations. Just let whatever arises be there without judgment, or if there is judgment there, just let it be and make note of it. When you're ready, write as briefly or as in depth on this reflection as you like.

_____

_____

_____

_____

_____

_____

Hope can reduce suffering and support resiliency in the face of life's challenges. It's a strength that we all have inside. What do you hope for? What do you hope will be different? What kind of life do you want to move toward?

_____

_____

_____

_____

_____

_____

_____

Getting in touch with what helps, what hasn't helped, and your hopes is a powerful step in your journey toward well-being. You may be remembering and even learning for the first time what is genuinely supportive to you. This will help you utilize these resources more consciously and effectively. Conversely, you may be realizing what doesn't serve you, which will help motivate you to refrain from ineffective strategies that bring further suffering and pain. Getting in touch with your hopes puts you in touch with a vision and your potential to blossom fully into who you want to be.

Before you move on, take a few moments to connect with your breath and mindfully reflect on what you just wrote, compassionately acknowledging, validating, and integrating everything you learned from this exploration.

---

mind traps

One major way that mindfulness helps with stress is by enabling you to observe the mind traps that may play a role in your stress or your reaction to stress. Mind traps are common mental habits that tend to exacerbate stress and pain. Once you've come to recognize these traps, you can more easily avoid falling into them. It may be that initially you'll only recognize them once you've fallen into them. But with time and practice, you'll be able to catch yourself before you're entirely ensnared. And eventually you'll be able to see these traps as you approach them—perhaps not every time, but often enough to make a real difference in your stress, well-being, and how you experience your life.

Negative Self-Talk

Self-talk is, naturally, the way you talk to yourself. It also refers to habitual styles of thinking and how you automatically interpret events. Unfortunately, this internal monologue is often negative. It's no secret that each of us is our own worst critic. People are often unbelievably hard on themselves. After doing something that you regret, you're likely to have thoughts such as "I'm such an idiot" or "I'm worthless," or you may even go so far as to think, "I hate myself." Maybe you analyze a single, regrettable action and make global assumptions like "I'll never get this right, no one can help me, and things will never change." Consider this: If a friend said these sorts of negative things about you, how would you feel? You might feel hopeless, sad, or angry, or you might not want to hang out with that person at all.

When feelings of stress, anxiety, or panic arise, it can be like wearing glasses that tend to distort reality and make it more worrisome. This keeps the anxious tape loops spinning in your head, exacerbating fears and possibly leading to panic. Take the internal thoughts "I'm not good enough," "Nobody understands me," and "I'll never find a partner." Mindlessly entertaining these thoughts and buying into them can lead to increased stress, anxiety, and depressed mood. The next thing you know, self-judgments start rising up, like "I'm unworthy and just a bad person," "No one will ever understand me because I'm different and odd and I don't belong," or "I'm the most undesirable person in the world. No one will find me attractive. No one is even interested in me." The beauty of mindfulness is that it can help you learn to treat thoughts, including these kinds of distressing thoughts, as mental events rather than facts.

When a thought pops into your mind, you can think of it as an event in the mind. You can become aware of it even as it arises and also notice as it eventually passes. In the same way that you can sit by a stream and watch leaves float by or look up at the sky watching the clouds come and go, while practicing mindfulness you'll learn to become more aware of all the stuff that's in your mind without attaching to it—just being aware of it as it comes and goes.

Habitual Styles of Thinking

In addition to letting negative self-talk run rampant, it's easy to get caught in habitual styles of thinking that can keep you feeling stuck and moody, which is obviously detrimental to your well-being. Because these thinking patterns often occur unconsciously, it's helpful to become familiar with them so you can be mindful of when you might be falling into these traps. Read the following descriptions of various negative thought patterns below and check off any that you might engage in. The purpose of this exercise isn't to judge yourself for the number of check marks, but simply to increase your awareness of a style of thinking that may be operating to keep you stuck. With this increased awareness comes the opportunity and the ability to choose to look at the situation differently or to view your thoughts as simply events, rather than as facts.

- ☐ **Catastrophizing** is a style of thinking that amplifies anxiety. In challenging situations, it expects disaster and automatically imagines the worst possible outcome. It's a what-if game of worst-case scenarios. An example would be telling someone that it's raining pretty hard, and they respond with "Yes, it seems like it will never stop. It's going to flood, and we're going to lose all our crops."

- ☐ **Exaggerating the negative** and **discounting the positive** go hand in hand and contribute to anxious and depressed moods as positive experiences are downplayed or not acknowledged while negative details are magnified. An example is when you say something positive, then use the word "but" to lead in to a negative statement, such as "I'm doing better at work, but I'm still making mistakes." This discounts the positive and gives more power to the negative. Experiment with replacing "but" with "and" to give both aspects equal weight.

- ☐ **Mind reading** involves convincing yourself that you know what other people are thinking and feeling and why they act the way they do, *without actual evidence*. For example, you may incorrectly assume that someone doesn't like you or is out to get you. Such interpretations tend to cultivate anxiety or depression.

- ☐ **Being the eternal expert** is a recipe for heightened stress, as it necessitates being constantly on guard. When being wrong isn't an option, you're continually on trial to defend your opinions and actions.

- ☐ **The "shoulds"** are an all-too-common thought pattern that can lead to guilt or anger in addition to stress. Shoulds involve having a list of unbreakable rules for yourself or others. If you break your rules for yourself, guilt often arises because you haven't lived up to your own expectations. If others break these rules, you're likely to become angry or resentful.

☐   **Blaming** involves holding others responsible for your own pain or holding yourself responsible for the problems of others. With blaming, there's always someone or something outside of yourself that's the cause of your suffering and pain. However, you generally can't change others, and you may not be able to change circumstances—you can only hope to change yourself. If you perceive that the solution lies outside of you, you deprive yourself of the power to effect change.

Allowing these types of thinking free rein is a recipe for stress, anxiety, and even depressed mood. Just being aware, without judgment, of your styles of thinking allows you to step outside of them and gain more insight into the inner workings of your mind. In other words, it will allow you to work more skillfully with your mind, instead of letting your mind control you.

Negative Interpretations

How you interpret events can have a tremendous effect on your level of stress. Read the following scenarios and notice your initial response. When a recent date doesn't call back, does that mean the romance is cooling, or that the person has been busy? Does getting a speeding ticket mean the world is out to get you, or that you need to slow down? Is showing your emotions a sign of weakness, or a sign of courage? It isn't at all unusual for the first response to be a negative interpretation, and this often happens so quickly or unconsciously that we don't realize we're doing it. However, this lack of awareness can keep you in a self-perpetuating cycle of anxious feelings and tense physical sensations. Again, mindfulness is the vehicle for noticing negative interpretations, and also the key to awareness of other options or interpretations. In fact, what seems like a disaster might actually be a gift.

Here's a story of a wise old man that illustrates this point. Everyone in the village looked up to this wise old man and sought his advice. One summer day, a farmer came to him in a state of panic and said, "Wise sage, I don't know what to do. My ox has died and now I'm unable to plow my fields. This is the worst thing that could ever have happened."

The sage looked him in the eye and replied, "Maybe so, maybe not." In a state of disbelief, the man returned to his family and proceeded to tell them how the sage was no sage after all and that he had lost his mind, because surely the death of the ox was the worst thing that could have happened.

The next morning the farmer went on a walk to think about how he would manage without the ox, and in the distance he saw a strong young horse grazing in the field. Immediately he had the idea that if he could catch the horse, his troubles would be over. Eventually he succeeded and brought the horse back. He realized how blessed he was because plowing was even easier than before. This reminded him of the sage, and at his first opportunity he went to see the sage and told him, "Please accept my apologies. You were absolutely right. If I hadn't lost my ox, I wouldn't have gone on that walk, and I never would have captured the horse. You have to agree that catching this horse was the best thing that ever happened."

The old sage looked into his eyes and said, "Maybe so, maybe not."

"Are you kidding me?" the farmer thought as he turned to leave. "This guy is a nut. I don't think I'll be coming by here again." A few days later the farmer's son was riding the horse and was bucked off. He broke his leg and was unable to help on the farm. "This is the worst thing that could ever have happened," thought the farmer. "How will we get by?" Realizing that the sage had spoken wisely in the past after all, the farmer went back to the sage and told him what had happened. "You must see the future. How did you know this would happen? I don't know how we'll get all the work done now. This time you have to admit, this is the worst thing that could ever have happened."

Once again, calmly and with love, the sage looked into the farmer's eyes and replied, "Maybe so, maybe not." The farmer was infuriated by this response and stormed back to the village.

The very next day, troops arrived in the village to enlist all healthy young men to fight in the ongoing and seemingly never-ending war. Because of his broken leg, the farmer's son was the only young man not taken, and thus he was spared from an almost certain death.

Just Do It!

Notice if there's any negative self-talk in your mind at this moment. You may hear thoughts like "This isn't going to work for me" or "Who am I kidding? Things will never change." If so, ask yourself if there's another way you can view the situation. What happens if you do as the sage in the story and say, "Maybe so, maybe not." Over the next week, take this practice with you into your daily life, looking out for automatic negative interpretations and other mind traps.

formal practice: Fifteen-Minute Mindful Breathing

This practice, a fifteen-minute version of the mindful breathing practice in chapter 3, will support you in bringing yourself back to the present moment with greater awareness, compassion, and peace. As such, it's a good antidote to all varieties of mind traps and therefore often serves as a starting point for the meditations in this book. Remember, at any point in time you can use the breath as an anchor to come back to the present moment. Simply focus attention solely upon the breath. Don't try to control it; just breathe normally and naturally, feeling it in the nose, belly, or wherever you feel it most prominently, being mindful of the breath rising as you inhale and falling as you exhale.

Do this practice in a relaxing environment without distractions, such as the phone. You can do it either lying down or sitting up, but if you lie down and find yourself falling asleep, try a more upright posture. Bring your full, undivided attention to this practice as you listen to track 4 on the enclosed CD or read the text below, pausing after each paragraph longer than you did in the five-minute breathing practice.

Take a few moments to be still. Congratulate yourself for taking some time for meditation practice.

Bring your awareness to your breath wherever you feel it most prominently in your body. It may be at the nose, neck, chest, belly, or somewhere else. As you breathe in normally and naturally, be aware of breathing in, and as you breathe out, be aware of breathing out. Simply maintain this awareness of the breath, breathing in and breathing out.

There is no need to visualize, count, or figure out the breath; just be mindful of breathing in and out. Without judgment, just watch the breath ebb and flow like waves in the sea. There's no place to go and nothing else to do, just be in the here and now, noticing the breath—just living life one inhalation and one exhalation at a time.

As you breathe in and out, be mindful of the breath rising on the inhalation and falling on the exhalation. Just riding the waves of the breath, moment by moment, breathing in and breathing out.

From time to time, attention may wander from the breath. When you notice this, simply acknowledge where you went and then gently bring your attention back to the breath.

Breathing normally and naturally, without manipulating the breath in any way, just be aware of the breath as it comes and goes.

As you come to the end of this meditation, congratulate yourself for taking this time to be present, realizing that this is an act of love. May we be at peace. May all beings be at peace.

Fifteen-Minute Mindful Breathing Journal

Take some time to write about whatever arose for you mentally, emotionally, and physically when doing this practice for the first time. How was it different for you than the five-minute practice?

_____

_____

_____

_____

_____

_____

_____

_____

formal practice: Walking Meditation

Mindful walking is an excellent way to get out of a stressful and anxious head and feel your feet on the earth. In everyday life, walking generally consists of going from point A to point B. You may feel that you're almost constantly on the go and on your feet. Walking meditation is different. It's deliberate and serves a different purpose than simply getting from point A to point B. With walking meditation, the point is to arrive in the present moment with each step.

If you have the ability to walk, you generally do so every day of your life and probably seldom bring much attention to it. Although it took a year or more for you to learn how to balance on your little feet as an infant, if you're like most people, once you started walking you never looked back, and now you probably take the ability to walk for granted. However, just think of the size of your body compared to the size of your feet. In a way, it's a miracle that we humans can balance and walk at all.

Walking meditation involves noticing the movement of each foot as you lift it, move it forward, and place it back down with each step. Although it's simple, initially you'll find it helpful to finish one step completely before lifting the other foot: "Lifting, moving, placing. Lifting, moving, placing." Slow the process down and use the movement to develop a careful awareness of your body. Over the course of a day, you can expect many changes. Sometimes you may feel like walking more quickly, sometimes very slowly. Whatever the situation and your inclination, place all of your attention on experiencing the movement and feeling the sensations of lifting, moving forward, and placing each foot back down. This is presented as a formal practice below, but you can practice mindful walking informally in everyday life. And like any of the practices in this book, you can practice for just a few minutes at a time, throughout your day.

Find a quiet place where you can walk undisturbed for about ten minutes without distractions, and where you can walk back and forth for a distance of ten to twenty feet. Bring your full, undivided attention to this practice as you listen to track 5 on the enclosed CD or read the text below and then begin the practice. Start off by walking slowly and paying attention to sensations on the soles of the feet as each part of the sole, from heel to toes, touches the ground. Notice how the body moves as you walk and how the arms may swing back and forth. If at any point you notice the mind wandering from walking, just acknowledge this and gently bring the focus back.

Begin standing and by taking a moment to feel into the body. Feel the connection of the body to the ground or the floor.

Become aware of your surroundings, spending a few moments taking in any sights, smells, tastes, sounds, or other sensations. Also note and acknowledge any thoughts and emotions, and let all of these sensations and internal experiences be.

Now mindfully begin to focus solely upon walking as you shift the weight to the left leg and begin to lift the right foot up, then move it forward, then place it back down on the ground.

And mindfully shift the weight to the right leg and begin to lift the left foot up, then move it forward, then place it back down on the ground.

Start off by walking slowly and paying attention to sensations on the soles of the feet as each part of the sole, from heel to toes, touches the ground. Notice how the body moves as you walk with your arms either swinging back and forth or clasped behind or in front of you.

Walk with awareness, one step at a time.

Continue walking one step at a time until you come to the designated end point. Without interrupting the flow of mindfulness, bring awareness to the intricate process of turning and beginning to walk back to where you started.

Walk with awareness one step at a time.

Continue walking, turning, and returning one step at a time.

Walk with mindfulness.

Walking Meditation Journal

As soon as you finish your first mindful walking practice, take a moment to write about any thoughts, feelings, and sensations you noticed during this meditation.

_____

_____

_____

_____

_____

_____

_____

informal practice: STOP

An informal way of using mindfulness to decrease stress and anxiety in daily life is encapsulated in the acronym STOP, which outlines a very simple and effective method for bringing the body and mind back into balance:

S = Stop.

T = Take a breath.

O = Observe.

P = Proceed.

There may be many times during the day when you're unaware of what's happening inside you. By taking a moment to stop, take a breath, and observe whatever is happening, including your own thoughts, emotions, and sensations, you can reconnect with your experience and then proceed and respond more effectively. This practice can be very revealing. Perhaps your shoulders are tense, your jaw is clenched, or your body is otherwise filled with tension. Perhaps you're hungry or tired or need a break. Maybe it's simply time to remind yourself to come back into the present moment. You can practice anytime you feel tense or upset, or anytime you like. You might choose to do this practice before or after certain activities, or you might even schedule various times during the day to STOP and check in with yourself. We know people who have used scheduling software to set a pop-up reminder once every hour. Be creative and find different ways to prompt yourself to STOP and come back into the moment. We each can become an active participant in the management of our own health and develop the potential to experience any moment, no matter how difficult or intense, with more balance and peace.

FAQ

Sometimes I feel angry, anxious, sad, confused, or afraid when I meditate. How do I accept or let go of my emotions?

First of all, you don't have to accept them. Acceptance implies being okay or at peace. Perhaps you can begin by acknowledging the feelings you're directly experiencing. Mindfulness encourages you to acknowledge your emotions rather than trying to accept them, no matter what they are, without any censorship. Begin by observing that the very resistance to emotional pain often causes more pain, and that learning to "go with it" rather than fighting it causes the very relationship with pain to change and often diminish. The notion of "going with the pain" means that you acknowledge whatever is felt within the mind and body. It's the act of just letting the waves of sensations and emotions go wherever they need to go and letting them be.

As far as letting go of emotions, we suggest putting your energy into learning to let them be. This is different from letting go. If you could figure out how to truly let go, life might be easier, but this is often difficult to do. By learning to let be, you begin to acknowledge the pain and provide a space for it to resonate in whatever direction it needs to go. When you learn to go with what's happening rather than fighting it, suffering and resistance often lessen. When meditating, try allowing the energy of fear or any emotion you feel in the body or mind to just be, without striving to change it or push it away. Knowing how these feelings manifest in your mind and body is valuable information. Outside of practice, you can use these sensations as cues that you're becoming fearful, anxious, or agitated. And as you sit with whatever emotion is there and the associated physical sensations, you'll come to understand that whatever arises, even difficult emotions and the associated physical sensations, does indeed pass away.

Planning and Reviewing Your Practice

Here are the formal practices from this chapter. Go ahead and put them on your calendar over the next week. Try to practice at least five days a week. Also schedule a time about a week from now when you'll review your practice to see how it's going.

Formal Practices

☐   Fifteen-Minute Mindful Breathing

☐   Walking Meditation

Now you have four informal practices to integrate into your daily life.

Informal Practices

☐   STOP

☐   Bringing the Eight Attitudes of Mindfulness into Your Life

☐   Weaving Mindfulness Throughout Your Day

☐   Mindful Eating

Formal Practice Log

Each time you do a formal practice, fill out the following log. As you fill it out, and as you look back over the previous week's practice, think about how your practice has been going. Do you notice any patterns about what works best for you? What changes could you make to sustain the discipline?

Date and practice	Time	Thoughts, feelings, and sensations that arose during this practice and how you felt afterward

Reflecting on Informal Practice

Take some time every day to reflect on at least one instance of informal practice. You can use what you learn from these reflections to deepen your daily informal practice.

Practice	What was the situation?	What did you notice before?	What did you notice after?	What did you learn?

mindfulness of the body

It's quite obvious that you need a body to live and that you won't get another one in this lifetime. You may perhaps have some parts surgically removed or replaced, but there's no such thing as a total body transplant. The body is the vehicle you live within through the journey of life, and you must care for it to promote its health, wellness, and longevity. Bringing mindfulness to the body can help you learn what your body does and doesn't need in order to thrive. It can also reveal a great deal about your world and your life. Through mindfulness of the body, you can begin to understand how stress and anxiety affect you, and also learn how to live better even with physical pain and illness. We'll help you open the door to greater mindfulness of the body using a time-honored practice: the body scan. We'll also explore how to work with physical pain, as well as the links between emotions and physical sensations and how you can use physical sensations as a key to your emotional state.

benefits of body awareness

The body scan meditation is a deep investigation into the moment-to-moment experiences of the body. By bringing awareness and acknowledgment to whatever you feel or sense in the body, the body scan can be very helpful in working with stress, anxiety, and physical pain. While you may have heard about meditations that create out-of-body experiences, the object of the body scan is to have an "in-the-body" experience. Most of us can benefit from developing this awareness. If you're like most people, you probably spend quite a bit of time living outside of your body while thinking of the future or past, imagining all sorts of scenarios, contemplating abstractions, or being otherwise preoccupied with your thoughts. In a short story entitled "A Painful Case," James Joyce wrote about Mr. Duffy, a man who "lived at a little distance from his body" (2006, 86). Can you identify with Mr. Duffy?

In the body scan, you methodically bring attention to the body, beginning with the left foot and ending at the top of the head. You may notice a wide range of physical feelings: itches, aches, tingles, pain, lightness, heaviness, warmth, cold, and more, as well as neutrality. Some of these sensations may be accompanied by thoughts or emotions. As you practice the body scan, this multitude of sensations and internal experiences can be boiled down to three basic feelings: pleasant, unpleasant, and neutral. Since the body is a dynamic organism that's always changing, no two body scans will ever be completely alike. But as you continue to practice, you'll discover what Martha Graham sagely noted: "The body says what words cannot" (Hanna 2006, 33). The body has its own wisdom, and if you listen, it can communicate where physical tension, thoughts, and emotions lie within your body. This investigation into physical sensations, thoughts, and emotions is sometimes called the triangle of awareness, since it's a journey into the totality of our human experience.

When you practice the body scan, first simply become aware of physical sensations by exploring their felt sense. This is distinct from thinking about your body. There's no need to analyze or manipulate your body in any way; just feel and acknowledge whatever sensations are present. Through this deep investigation, the body may begin to reveal a whole range of feelings. In this way, the body scan can bring you in touch with many aspects of your life.

---

formal practice: Body Scan

The body scan is a wonderful way to get in touch with your body and mind. Do this practice in a relaxing environment without distractions. We suggest lying down while doing the body scan, but if you find yourself sleepy or would just rather sit or stand, you are welcome to do that too. Bring your full, undivided attention to this practice as you listen to the CD. Try to do the full forty-five-minute practice (track 8). However, if you're short on time, the CD also includes a thirty-minute version (track 7) and a fifteen-minute version (track 6). If you're reading the text, pause after each paragraph to make the exercise last forty-five, thirty, or fifteen minutes.

Take a few moments to be still. Congratulate yourself for taking this time for meditation practice.

Do a mindful check-in, feeling into your body and mind and simply allowing any waves of thoughts, emotions, and physical sensations to just be.

Perhaps it's been a busy day and this is the first time you're stopping. As you begin to enter the world of being rather than doing, you may notice the trajectory of the feelings you've been carrying within you.

There is no need to judge, analyze, or figure things out. Just allow yourself to be in the moment with all that's there.

When you feel ready, gently shift the focus to the breath.

Now become aware of breathing.

Breathe normally and naturally and focus on the tip of the nose or the abdomen. Breathing in and knowing you're breathing in, and breathing out and knowing you're breathing out.

At times the mind may wander away from awareness of breathing. When you recognize this, acknowledge wherever you went and then come back to the breath, breathing in and out with awareness.

And now gently withdraw awareness from mindful breathing as you shift to the body scan. As you go through the body, you may come across areas that are tight or tense. If you can allow them to soften, let that happen; if you can't, just let the sensations be, letting them ripple in whatever direction they need to go. This applies not only to physical sensations but also to any emotions. As you go through the body be mindful of any physical sensations and any thoughts or emotions that may arise from sensations.

Bring awareness to the bottom of the left foot where you feel the contact of your foot on the floor. It could be the back of the heel or the bottom of the left foot. Sensing into what is being felt. Feeling the heel, ball, and sole of the left foot.

Feel into your toes and the top of the left foot and back into the Achilles tendon and up into the left ankle.

Now move your awareness up to the lower left leg, feeling into the calf and shin and their connection to the left knee. Being present.

Let awareness now rise up to the thigh, sensing into the upper leg and its connection above into the left hip.

And now withdraw awareness from the left hip down to the left foot, shifting it into the right foot and bringing awareness to where you feel the contact of your right foot on the floor. It could be the back of the heel or the bottom of the right foot. Sensing into what is being felt. Feeling the heel, ball, and sole of the right foot.

Feel into the toes and the top of the right foot and back into the Achilles tendon and up into the right ankle.

Now move your awareness up to the lower right leg, feeling into the calf and shin and their connection to the right knee. Being present.

Let awareness now rise up into the thigh, sensing into the upper leg and its connection above into the right hip.

Gently withdraw your attention from the right hip and move into the pelvic region. Sense into the systems of elimination, sexuality, and reproduction. Feeling into the genitals and the anal region. Being mindful to any sensations, thoughts, or emotions.

And now lift the awareness to the abdomen and into the belly, the home of digestion and assimilation, feeling into your guts with awareness and letting be.

Now withdraw your awareness from the belly and move to the tailbone and begin to sense into the lower, middle, and upper parts of the back. Feeling sensations. Allow any tightness to soften and let be what's not softening.

Let the awareness now shift into the chest, into the heart and lungs. Being present. Feeling into the rib cage and sternum and then into the breasts.

Now gently withdraw attention from the chest and shift the awareness into the fingertips of the left hand. Feeling into the fingers and palm, and then the back of the hand and up into the left wrist.

Proceed up into the forearm, elbow, and upper left arm, feeling sensations.

Now shift awareness to the fingertips of the right hand. Feeling into the fingers and palm, and then the back of the hand and up into the right wrist.

Proceed up into the forearm, elbow, and upper right arm, feeling sensations.

Let the awareness move into both shoulders and armpits and then up into the neck and throat. Being present to any sensations, thoughts or emotions.

Now bring your awareness into the jaw and then gently into the teeth, tongue, mouth, and lips. Allowing any resonating sensations to go wherever they need to go and letting be.

Feel into the cheeks, the sinus passages that go deep into the head, the eyes, and the muscles around the eyes. Feel into the forehead and the temples, being present.

Let the awareness move into the top and back of the head. Feeling into the ears and then inside of the head and into the brain. Being present.

Now expand the field of awareness to the entire body from head to toe to fingertips. Connect from the head through the neck to the shoulders, arms, hands, chest, back, belly, hips, pelvic region, legs, and feet.

Feel the body as a whole organism, with its various physical sensations, thoughts, and emotions. Being present.

Breathing in, feel the whole body rising and expanding on an inhalation and falling and contracting on an exhalation. Feel the body as a whole organism. Being present.

As you come to the end of the body scan, congratulate yourself for taking this time to be present. May you know that this is an act of love.

May all beings be at peace.

Body Scan Journal

It's truly amazing when you get in touch with your body and discover where you're feeling and harboring stress and tension and where various emotions may reside. As you sense into the body, a myriad of feelings, thoughts, and experiences may emerge. It's also important to know that sometimes you might not feel much of anything, and that this too can be explored. What does nothing or a neutral state feel like? As you feel into the body, acknowledge and validate all experiences, barring none. Many of us often experience unexplainable aches and pains. By practicing the body scan, you may discover that these reflect your tension or emotions, perhaps stored in your chest, neck, jaw, shoulders, back, or stomach. Did the body scan help you become more aware of where you carry tension or emotions in the body? Take a moment to note whether you felt stress, anxiety, elation, sadness, joy, anger, or any other emotion in the body. Write about whatever came up for you mentally, emotionally, and physically when doing this practice for the first time.

_____

_____

_____

_____

_____

_____

_____

_____

FAQ

Am I doing the body scan right if I don't feel anything?

It's important to know that neutral sensations can be part of the body scan. Human beings generally feel three types of sensations: pleasant, unpleasant, and neutral. If you're experiencing a neutral sensation, simply be mindful that it's neutral. As you deepen your practice of the body scan, you may begin to be aware of more and more subtle feelings. It's like when you go to the ocean and initially only hear the loud crashing of the waves; after some time you may distinguish smaller and more subtle sounds that make up the overall crashing. So it is with the body scan. As you deepen your practice, you'll begin to feel more and more sensations.

how to work with physical pain

We all experience physical pain from time to time. If you have a chronic pain problem, that may be part of the reason you're working with this book. Or perhaps as you worked with the body scan, you became aware that you have pain or that you habitually hold tension in certain parts of your body. The first step in working with pain is to assess whether it's acute or chronic. Acute pain usually has a physical cause and is often associated with a recent injury or physical problem. It may require immediate medical attention. While chronic pain may also have a physical cause, it's likely to be associated with cognitive and emotional components, as well, such as grief, anger, fear, or confusion.

Mindfulness meditation has been shown to be helpful with chronic pain (Kabat-Zinn et al. 1986). There are three important steps in applying mindfulness to chronic pain. The first is investigation—sensing into your body and feeling how you hold tension and pain. The second is working with any emotional reactions to the pain and tension. The third involves taking a more philosophical approach—learning to live in the here and now and dealing with pain one moment at a time.

Step 1: Investigating Pain and Tension in the Body

It may sound counterintuitive or even frightening to bring focused attention to the body and its sensations when you're feeling pain. Isn't it normal and natural to want to escape or distract yourself from pain? Why would you want to bring awareness to discomfort when it seems so much better to get rid of it? However, if you don't know how you're holding pain and tension in the body, you may be increasing it inadvertently. This is where mindfulness comes in.

A common knee-jerk reaction to pain is to clench and get tighter around it. Unfortunately, this can not only increase the physical pain, it may also begin a vicious cycle of reactions that lead to increased anger, fear, sadness, and confusion. Getting tight around pain further constricts the muscles and restricts blood flow, which may cause more spasms and pain, possibly even in other areas of the body. This cycle is difficult to stop, and in time you may discover that you're constricted not just around the painful area, but throughout the body.

The body scan provides an opportunity for you to reorient toward living and working with tension and pain. As you reeducate yourself about your pain by distinguishing physical sensations from mental and emotional feelings, you can learn to recognize strong sensations in the body as just physical sensations. That said, living with physical tension and pain can be very difficult and cause high levels of stress and anxiety, so it's important to learn some skills for both coping with pain and learning to reduce it.

Once you become aware of how you hold pain in the body, you can start figuring out how best to work with it. For example, you may have lower back pain and, using the body scan, discover that the tension and tightness expands up to the top of the head—that your entire upper body is a constricted mass of pain. Is there a need for the extra tension and tightness beyond the low back area? The truth is, you may be further exacerbating your pain by holding this musculoskeletal tension.

So how do you deal with this extensive area of constricted tension and pain? Mindful awareness will not only allow you to see where you're holding unnecessary tension, but will also help you soften and possibly release tension in these areas where there's no pain at all. Mindfulness also teaches that if you can't release the tension, you can practice riding its waves, just observing them, letting them be, and allowing them to ripple wherever they need to go. Just like watching ripples in a pond extend out farther and farther, you can give space to sensations and let them go wherever they need to go. Learning to be with pain may feel counterintuitive, but it's a fundamental step in healing. Rather than investing your energy in fighting or resisting pain, learn to go with it. This is an ancient wisdom that goes back to the Buddha, who taught that whenever there is resistance to what is, there's suffering.

Step 2: Working with the Emotions in Physical Pain

Why is it that we have such a hard time dealing with physical and emotional pain? Is it because of our upbringing? Do we live in a culture that prefers to deny the existence of pain? We certainly receive many cultural messages that encourage us to keep a stiff upper lip and suppress, repress, avoid, or deny our pain and other feelings.

Mindfulness, on the other hand, offers a pathway to working with the uncomfortable emotions that often arise when you have physical pain, such as anger, rage, sadness, confusion, despair, grief, anxiety, and fear. Bringing mindful awareness to emotions allows you to begin to acknowledge them, no matter what they are, validating and acknowledging them without censorship and without resistance. As with physical pain, resistance to difficult emotions often causes more pain, while learning to let be and go with them, rather than fighting them, can often diminish or change the suffering associated with them. Rather than fighting difficult emotions, simply allow and acknowledge whatever you feel, letting the waves of emotion go wherever they need to go.

As mentioned earlier, there are important distinctions between "acknowledgment" and "acceptance," and between "letting be" and "letting go." To "acknowledge" is to simply see things as they are, whether you like it or not. "Acceptance," on the other hand, can be seen as being okay or at peace with things as they are. If you're experiencing pain, it may be difficult to be okay with the pain, but you can acknowledge it even if you don't accept it. Likewise, "letting be" is different from "letting go." "Letting go" implies being able to release, whereas "letting be" simply provides space for things to be as they are. Just like the sky gives space to a storm, you can give space to your emotions.

Acknowledging emotional pain helps create the possibility for deeper understanding, compassion, and peace. As you gain more understanding of your physical pain, your emotional reactions to it, and the differences between them, you'll begin to see that there's a difference between physical pain and suffering. Even in times when you can't change the physical sensations of pain, you can change your emotional responses to them and thereby reduce your suffering. In other words, physical pain is a reality, but suffering is optional. The body does have pain receptors and is designed to feel pain; in fact, in some cases it can help prevent injury. However, your emotional response to pain is in your hands. With time and practice, you can learn to feel the pain and suffer less.

Step 3: Living in the Present Moment

The third step is living in the present moment. The truth is, you can only live in the here and now. This is the only moment in which you can make any changes. When you identify with stress, tension, or chronic pain, you may think of it as a long-term problem or life sentence, and this attitude can take you out of the present moment and increase your suffering. Mindfulness teaches you to be here now. You don't know what the future may bring, and you really don't know if the stress and pain will last forever. Through mindfulness practice, you can learn to be with pain one moment at a time and develop an attitude of "Let's see if I can be with pain in this moment. If pain arises in the next moment, I'll deal with it then."

As you deepen your practice of mindfulness, you'll reconnect to yourself and discover new strategies to work with tension and pain. Rather than being held hostage by your discomfort, you can cultivate the attitude that it's possible to learn from it. As you learn to let go of the past and not to cling to a specific vision of the future, you'll be able to see things as they are in the moment, with a growing sense of freedom and the possibility of new options. This perspective transforms you, your pain, and your relationship to your pain.

informal practice: Minding Your Pain

When we experience stress, tension, emotional pain, or chronic physical pain, most of us have an immediate reaction to try to get away from the unpleasant feeling. However, you also have the option of choosing to relate to it in a different way by bringing attention to how you're holding it in the body in the moment. If you can allow the area to soften, that's fine. If not, see if you can adopt the attitude of mindfulness, just riding the waves of sensations and letting them be.

As an informal practice, throughout the next week bring attention to physical sensations or emotions in your body and just notice how you're feeling. Bring beginner's mind or gentle curiosity to the feeling, cradling it in your awareness and just letting it be. Allow yourself to experience these physical or emotional sensations and allow them to be as they are, without resistance or judgment. To help you remember to practice, you could schedule a pop-up reminder in an electronic calendar that says something like "How is my body?"

emotions in the body

The body scan can help you get in touch with difficult, daunting, and even overwhelming emotions. The first step is to learn to identify these feelings more readily so that you can work with them more creatively. Take anxiety, for example. If you're unaware of anxiety in the moment, it could be influencing your behavior in ways that actually increase anxiety instead of relieving it. The body scan can also help you tune in to physical sensations that can serve as a signpost as to whether certain emotions are present. With anxiety, you may notice tightness in the chest, tension in the shoulders or back, or cramping in the stomach. You can use awareness of these sensations to alert you that you might be anxious, allowing you to work with that emotion before it snowballs.

Here's a true story that illustrates this point. Joe lost several family members in an automobile accident and felt as if he had lost his ability to smile. He became so self-conscious about this that when others began to smile at him, he immediately turned away and looked down. When his therapist asked how his body felt when people smiled at him, Joe said he didn't notice anything. So in session, they worked on Joe becoming more aware of the physical sensations in his body through the body scan. His therapist then led Joe through an imaginary experience of walking down the street and noticing people smiling at him. During this visualization, his therapist encouraged him to notice physical sensations in his body. Joe became aware of tightness in his chest, tension in his shoulders, and his neck turning as his head fell downward. Joe came to understand that these physical sensations signaled his unconscious reaction cycle of fear, self-judgment, and looking away.

As Joe continued to practice the body scan, he became more alert to these physical sensations and began to notice them occurring when he actually was walking down the street. Soon he was able to use the sensations as a signal to step out of his unconscious reaction, become present, and choose a different response. He chose to turn his head toward people who smiled at him and began to practice smiling back. Soon his smiles became more spontaneous, which led to encouraging thoughts, feelings of excitement, and relief from chronic tension and tightness in his body.

 ### *Bob's Story: Ben's Ouch!*

Some years ago my young son, Ben, fell down some stairs and bumped his head. Fortunately, he wasn't seriously injured, but it was painful and he didn't like it. He cried vociferously and was pretty mad, and a couple of friends came over to help. One friend pulled a piece of candy from his pocket and said, "Here you go, Ben. Eat this candy and you'll feel better." I thanked my friend and asked him to not give Ben the candy, since I felt crying was a reasonable response. The second friend came over and started making funny faces at Ben, trying to make him laugh, and said "You'll be okay, Ben." I thanked him as well, then asked him to not try to make Ben laugh, again explaining that Ben's response of crying was appropriate after bumping his head.

Ben continued to cry and rant, and I just held him and acknowledged and validated his pain. Ben told me, "Daddy, it hurts when you bump your head." I responded by saying, "Yes Ben, it does hurt when you bump your head." Eventually, Ben became quiet, and at some point he looked up at me and said, "C'mon Dad, let's get going."

Driving home, I realized that I had witnessed a completed experience. Ben didn't need to process this bumping on the head any further. It was finished on those steps. On the other hand, if I'd allowed him to have the candy or erase his pain with laughter and began to do this every time he had pain, Ben would have learned that it wasn't okay to cry and be angry. When we suppress or repress our feelings, the effect can be detrimental to our health and well-being.

barriers to awareness of emotions

There are a number of barriers to awareness of emotions, with four being especially noteworthy. The first barrier is that sometimes emotions are invalidated or otherwise discounted. If this happened while you were growing up, and you were told there was no reason to be anxious, fearful, sad, or angry when that's how you felt, it may have taught you not only to think that you aren't the best judge of your own emotions, but also that you should repress them. Emotions are meant to come and go like everything else. When they're constrained or repressed, it creates stress in the mind and body.

The second barrier to being aware of emotions is the common error of confusing thoughts with emotions. Whenever you say, "I feel that…," you're probably actually about to describe a thought or judgment, rather than an emotion. For example, a client named Julie used to say, "I feel that my life is out of control." As she learned to make a distinction between thoughts and feelings, she became aware that "out of control" is a thought, not a feeling. She began to notice that emotions of anxiety and confusion were connected to the thought "out of control," and that they also manifested in her body, as tension in her chest and shoulders. She used this as a signal of her emotional state and a reminder to turn her awareness to differentiating between thoughts and emotions. When Julie felt anxious and then actually looked at the evidence for her life being out of control, she realized that she was actually in control of many aspects of her life.

To further clarify this point, consider statements like "I feel stupid," "I feel worthless," or "I feel helpless." Again, the *thought* may be I'm stupid (or worthless or helpless), but the emotion would be something like shame, sadness, or fear. When thoughts are confused with emotions, it's often because the emotions are masked behind thoughts in an unconscious attempt to protect yourself from awareness of the emotion. A big advantage to developing the capacity to see the difference between the thought and the feeling behind it is that it allows you to look at the credibility of the thought that's hijacking you by coloring the way you see the world and digging you deeper into stress, anxiety, and possibly depression.

A third barrier to awareness of emotions is that they're intangible and therefore challenging to define. You learned that a flower is a flower because at some point someone pointed it out to you and told you the name. You could feel it, see it, and touch it. But no one can definitively point to a feeling of fear, sadness, or guilt, so as you were growing up, you had to experience and decipher these on your own.

The fourth barrier is that most of us simply don't have an adequate vocabulary in regard to emotions. Many of us grew up in a culture where experiencing and discussing emotions wasn't encouraged and therefore we didn't learn to describe feelings. The next exercise will help you develop a richer emotional vocabulary and greater awareness of how specific emotions manifest in your body.

---

explore: Identifying Emotions in the Body

It's sometimes said that there are just a handful of basic emotions, with all other emotions being variations on these basic themes. While this doesn't adequately address the complexity of the situation, it does provide some structure for becoming more familiar with the diversity of emotions. In this exercise, we've grouped both comfortable and uncomfortable emotions into categories to provide a springboard for developing a broader emotional vocabulary and bringing more awareness to your emotions. As you read through the lists below, circle the emotions that seem more familiar to you. Then write about where in your body you feel these emotions, how they manifest, and what thoughts or images come to mind as you read these emotion words. It may take some time to develop sensitivity to emotions and how they manifest in your body. If you aren't able to connect a specific emotion with bodily sensations or you can't think of anything to write about it, know that you can always come back and do this later.

Fear: apprehension, anxiety, distress, edginess, jumpiness, nervousness, panic, tenseness, uneasiness, worry, fright, feeling overwhelmed.

_____

_____

_____

_____

_____

_____

_____

Confusion: bewildered, uncertain, puzzled, mystified, perplexed, chaotic, foggy, or unaware.

_____

_____

_____

_____

_____

_____

_____

_____

Anger: aggravation, agitation, annoyance, destructiveness, disgust, envy, frustration, irritation, grouchiness, grumpiness, rage.

_____

_____

_____

_____

_____

_____

_____

Sadness: alienation, anguish, despair, disappointment, gloom, grief, hopelessness, insecurity, loneliness, misery, unhappiness, rejection.

_____

_____

_____

_____

_____

_____

_____

Shame: guilt, embarrassment, humiliation, invalidation, regret, remorse, mortification.

_____

_____

_____

_____

_____

_____

_____

Love: affection, arousal, attraction, caring, compassion, desire, fondness, infatuation, kindness, liking, longing, warmth, sympathy, sentimentality.

_____

_____

_____

_____

_____

_____

_____

_____

_____

Joy: amusement, bliss, contentment, eagerness, elation, enjoyment, enthusiasm, excitement, exhilaration, hope, optimism, pleasure, satisfaction.

_____

_____

_____

_____

_____

_____

_____

Noticing where emotions reside in the body may not come naturally. Know that as you continue to practice the body scan, you'll become more sensitive to physical sensations and how they relate to your emotions. From time to time, reread the lists in this exercise and watch for all of these different shades of emotion as you go about your daily life. When a strong emotion arises, try to take a moment to mindfully tune in to your body to discover any physical sensations associated with that emotion.

Before you move on, take a moment to connect with your breath and mindfully reflect on what you just wrote, compassionately acknowledging, validating, and integrating what you learned from this exploration.

 ## Elisha's Story: Approaching Emotions

While I used to pride myself on being aware of my emotions, in reality I've had difficulty in this area. Without my realizing it, sometimes when sadness or anger would arise, my nervous system viewed the emotion as a threat. My unconscious reaction was to change the subject, try to fix the situation, or just turn on the television—in other words, avoiding at all costs. When my wife suggested that I sometimes try to avoid uncomfortable emotions, I denied it. After all, I felt I had done a lot of work on self-awareness.

Still, over the years I've learned that my wife is often right, and as I sat with the idea, I began to realize that whether I was with friends, family, or an acquaintance, at times my body would stiffen up or my face would become tense, and I'd look for any opportunity to avoid being truly present in the interaction. As I observed this reaction and investigated what lay beneath it, I realized that this usually happened when I wanted to avoid a potentially painful interaction, and that this happened most often with the people I was closest to. This makes sense, as those relationships generally have the greatest potential to cause pain.

With this series of insights, I realized that I could use the stiffness that arose in my body or tension in my face as a cue that I was uncomfortable. But then I hit an impasse. My emotional vocabulary was limited, and the only words I could come up with to describe my emotional state were "uncomfortable" and "pain." So I worked on building my vocabulary of emotions and began to see that I was actually feeling edginess, jumpiness, and apprehension—all feelings associated with fear. As I deepened my exploration, I could feel the fear burning in my chest, right over my heart. Then an image flashed in my mind of a little boy inside of me, peeking through a crack in a wall and saying, "Oh no, I'm not going out there." I felt great sadness and compassion in response to the hurt and pain of that little boy inside of me.

In time, I could feel the impulse to pull away from connecting with others even as it arose, which allowed me to acknowledge the impulse and then bring my awareness back to experiencing the fear—not judging it as good or bad, just letting it be and staying connected. This has been immensely healing for me, and for my relationships.

Just Do It!

Right now, take a moment to check in with how you're feeling in your body. Is it sending you any signals about your emotions or thoughts? Is there any tension, tiredness, or tightness, or do you feel just right? Notice what arises when you become mindful of your body and its messages, and listen closely. Your body may be trying to communicate important information to you.

How Stressed Are You?

Congratulations! You've made it halfway through the book. What a wonderful gift, to have given yourself this time to become more present to your life. Before reading on, take a moment to go back to the exercise "What's Stressing You?" at the end of the introduction on page 11. Take this opportunity to revisit the stressors you wrote down at that time and assess how you're doing with them now.

Try to make this a mindful process. Before diving in with scoring, take a moment to breathe and check in with your body. Then take some time to think about each stressor and see if you feel differently or the same about it. If any new stressors arose since you first did the exercise, add them to the list and rate them as well.

This informal assessment isn't meant to replace a clinical assessment; it's simply intended to help you determine how you're feeling. However, if most of your ratings are extremely high, it would probably be a good idea to use this book in conjunction with a health care or mental health professional.

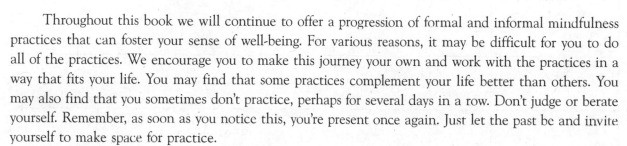

Planning and Reviewing Your Practice

Throughout this book we will continue to offer a progression of formal and informal mindfulness practices that can foster your sense of well-being. For various reasons, it may be difficult for you to do all of the practices. We encourage you to make this journey your own and work with the practices in a way that fits your life. You may find that some practices complement your life better than others. You may also find that you sometimes don't practice, perhaps for several days in a row. Don't judge or berate yourself. Remember, as soon as you notice this, you're present once again. Just let the past be and invite yourself to make space for practice.

In addition to practicing the body scan over the next week, we recommend that you continue to practice mindful walking at least five days a week. It's an excellent way to extend the approaches in this chapter to the body in motion. Go ahead and put these two practices on your calendar for the next week. Try to practice daily or near daily. Also schedule a time about a week from now when you'll review your practice to see how it's going.

Formal Practices

☐ Body Scan

☐ Walking Meditation

Now you have five informal practices to integrate into your daily life.

Informal Practices

☐ Minding Your Pain

☐ STOP

☐ Bringing the Eight Attitudes of Mindfulness into Your Life

☐ Weaving Mindfulness Throughout Your Day

☐ Mindful Eating

Formal Practice Log

Each time you do a formal practice, fill out the following log. As you fill it out, and as you look back over the previous week's practice, think about how your practice has been going. Do you notice any patterns about what works best for you? What changes could you make to sustain the discipline?

Date and Formal Practice	Time	Thoughts, feelings, and sensations that arose during this practice and how you felt afterward

Reflecting on Informal Practice

Take some time every day to reflect on at least one instance of informal practice. You can use what you learn from these reflections to deepen your daily informal practice.

Practice	What was the situation?	What did you notice before?	What did you notice after?	What did you learn?

deepening your practice

In chapter 3, we began to introduce you to the formal practice of mindfulness meditation. We outlined eight attitudes essential to mindfulness practice, introduced mindful breathing, talked about what to do when the mind wanders as it inevitably will, and gave specific recommendations on physical posture for formal practice. The formal practice in that chapter was five minutes of mindful breathing. In chapter 5, we focused on the body scan. All of this laid the foundation for the focus of this chapter: formal sitting practice of mindfulness meditation, which begins with mindfulness of breathing and gradually expands to physical sensations, sounds, thoughts and emotions, and ultimately choiceless awareness, also known as present moment awareness. Because extended sitting meditation can lead to stiffness, this chapter also includes a mindful yoga practice to help you work out the kinks while also deepening your mindfulness of the body and mind and their interconnections. As you deepen your mindfulness practice with sitting meditation, you'll become more aware of your thoughts and feelings, and also more aware of habitual patterns of behavior that may not serve you well. Looking at your behavior in this way, with beginner's mind, allows you to see that other possibilities exist—an important first step in choosing to do something different.

formal sitting mindfulness meditation

Outwardly, the formal practice of sitting mindfulness meditation is much like the popular conception of meditation: sitting in silent contemplation. You'll soon discover that the practice is quite rich and profound, as you turn your awareness to the ever-changing nature of your experience. By focusing on how the breath, sensations, sounds, thoughts, and emotions are continually forming and then falling away, it allows a glimpse of the transitory nature of all things—and the potential freedom that comes with this awareness. As you simply sit with and acknowledge whatever is with beginner's mind, without evaluation or judgment and without striving for a particular outcome, you'll develop greater equanimity, a deeper capacity for letting be, and, with time and practice, greater wisdom and compassion. As mentioned, this practice begins with a focus on the breath and expands outward to sensations, sounds, thoughts and emotions, and finally choiceless awareness. Let's take a closer look at each of these practices.

Mindfulness of Breathing

Sitting meditation often begins with mindfulness of breathing. By being aware of the shifting quality of the breath as you inhale and exhale, you can learn a great deal about the nature of impermanence and life. Much like the ebb and flow of the ocean's waves, the breath is constantly in a state of change, coming in and going out. This is a powerful teacher that underscores how everything changes in life and that it's possible to go with the flow rather than fighting it. It also brings a recognition that the stronger the resistance, the greater the suffering. It's natural to go after what you want and try to hold on to it and, conversely, to push away what you don't want. However, this self-limiting definition often fuels a push-and-pull relationship between what you want and don't want and can make you feel restless and ill at ease; in short, it leads to suffering. For example, if you try to resist the process of breathing, you'll find that discomfort arises almost instantly and can rapidly develop into suffering! Simply being with your breath as you practice mindfulness meditation allows you to experience firsthand the ever-changing quality of your experience and helps you open to going with the flow of life with less grasping and aversion and with a greater sense of space and freedom.

Mindfulness of Sensations

After spending some time with the breath, you'll expand your awareness to the field of physical sensations. This is different from the body scan. Rather than methodically going through the body part by part, you open awareness to whatever sensations are predominant or distinct in each moment. Noticing the coming and going of sensations throughout the body in this way makes this practice much more fluid and reflective of the direct experience of the present moment. The human body is a dynamic organism with sensory receptors that are essentially in a perpetual state of fluctuation, experiencing a wide array of sensations (itching, tingling, warmth, coolness, dryness, moisture, heaviness, lightness, pain, and so on) that may be either pleasant, unpleasant, or neutral. If you aren't feeling any distinct sensations, you can bring awareness to any points of contact, such as your body touching the chair, your feet on the floor, or your hands making contact with your lap—wherever you feel contact. In mindfulness meditation, there's nothing to analyze or figure out about these sensations. Simply maintain attention on the field of sensory experience, noticing as each sensation arises and then recedes. Directly focusing on the transitory quality of physical sensations will deepen your understanding of the nature of change.

Mindfulness of Hearing

Next, you'll extend your mindful awareness to hearing. By listening to various sounds rise and fall, you come into direct contact with impermanence in yet another way. Mindfulness of sounds can be very useful. As with mindfulness of the breath, most of us can engage in this practice almost anytime and anywhere, since so many of us live in noisy, busy environments where sounds are almost always coming and going. If a particular sound is persistent and possibly even annoying, such as a car alarm, loud music, kids screaming, traffic, or airplanes, simply bring attention to the sound itself without evaluation. On a more elemental level, the mind simply hears sound waves. Auditory phenomena are ever-present; you cannot escape them. Even if you isolated yourself in a deep cave or a soundproof room, you'd still hear internal sounds of your pulse, your heartbeat, or ringing in the ears. Whatever our audio environment, try not to judge the sounds as good or bad. Simply notice how sounds arise and recede as impermanent events.

As you turn your focus to hearing, you can begin to transform any irritation with sounds. There is no need to like or dislike them; they're just sounds. You may hear sounds outside or indoors, or as your concentration deepens, you may be aware of sounds within the body. All of these are just sounds, appearing and disappearing. There's no need to analyze or figure out these sounds; simply maintain bare attention on the ever-changing field of auditory experience.

Mindfulness of Thoughts and Emotions

After meditating on sounds, you'll shift to mental events (thoughts and emotions) as the object of meditation, directing attention to the mind and the thought process itself. As well as seeing and experiencing the content of your thoughts and emotions, sometimes known as the ten thousand joys and sorrows, you'll begin to see that thoughts and emotions are ever-changing, just like the breath, sensations, and sounds. Rather than getting involved in the contents of the mind, you can become more interested in just experiencing the process. As you become aware of the stories you spin and the traps you create, you can begin to disengage from them.

Mindfulness cultivates the ability to observe and experience thoughts and emotions as they arise, develop, and recede. There's no need to analyze them or figure them out; simply view them as mental formations that come and go. It's like lying in a meadow watching the clouds float through the sky or like sitting in a movie theater watching the images and sounds changing on the screen. In other words, the practice is to simply experience and be mindful of the changing nature of mental formations that rise and fall away moment to moment.

Here's a helpful metaphor: Many different types of storms arise in the ever-changing atmosphere of our planet—occasionally very powerful storms, such as Category 5 hurricanes. Yet even with the strongest hurricane, the sky doesn't feel the effect of the storms. The virtue of the sky is that it has plenty of space to let the storm run its course. Within this vast space, the storm eventually dissipates. In a sense, mindfulness helps you develop an internal awareness as big as the sky. By practicing mindfulness, you can begin to watch the storms of fear, anxiety, and other emotions and give them the space they need to transform and diminish in intensity. By observing and experiencing thoughts and emotions and allowing them to go wherever they need to go, you can come to see them as transient mental phenomena and understand that you are not your thoughts. Your thoughts are not facts, nor are they a complete definition of who you are. Freeing yourself from your own self-limiting constructions will bring deeper levels of freedom and peace.

Choiceless Awareness

The last and most expansive aspect of this practice of sitting mindfulness meditation is choiceless awareness, or present moment awareness. In this practice, the present moment becomes the primary object of attention. Choiceless awareness invites you to become mindful of whatever is arising in the unfolding of each moment in the endless succession of present moments—whatever arises in the body and mind, whether sensations, sounds, or other sensory phenomenon, or mental events like thoughts and emotions. Although outwardly you may be very still, your internal experience may be very different as you sit back and watch the ever-shifting tides of physical and mental experience.

Together, your body and mind are a single dynamic organism that's constantly in a state of change, with interactions between stimuli from thoughts, emotions, physical sensations, sounds, sights, smells, and tastes. As you practice choiceless awareness, simply observe what's predominant or compelling in the mind and body and be present to it. If nothing is especially prevalent and you're unsure of where to place your attention, you can always go back to the breath, sensations, sounds, or thoughts and emotions as a way to anchor into the here and now.

This practice is analogous to sitting by the edge of a river, just watching whatever goes downstream, and indeed, it is one of the most fluid of meditation practices as it reflects the unfolding of your direct experience, moment by moment. Sometimes there are sounds, sometimes sensations, sometimes thoughts and emotions. Just sit and witness the sea of change in your mind and body. Even if you're experiencing storms of anxiety, pain, sadness, anger, or confusion, know that by giving them space they will gradually diminish.

FAQ

I take my thoughts so seriously. What can I do about this?

Mindfulness teaches that thoughts and emotions are transitory. Just as physical sensations are constantly changing, the mind also is in a state of flux. Begin to observe the changing physical sensations of sounds, tastes, smells, sights, and touch, and come to see them as waves—formations that come into existence, rising up and then receding or falling away. The same is true of thoughts and emotions. Many people who practice mindfulness consider the mind to be a sense organ. Just like the nose smells, the tongue tastes, the body feels, the ears hear, and the eyes see, the mind thinks. This is just what it does. As you start to sense and acknowledge the impermanent nature of all things, you'll come to see that each moment genuinely does offer the opportunity for a new outlook or a new beginning. This is a position of immense freedom, and perhaps one of the greatest benefits of meditation: that we become less deeply enslaved by the mind. If you continue to struggle with attachment or aversion to certain thoughts or with taking them too seriously, sit or lie outside and look up at the clouds floating by. Imagine yourself as the sky and thoughts as clouds, and know that thoughts come and go, just as clouds do.

formal practice: Sitting Meditation

Sit in a posture that's comfortable yet allows you to remain alert. Bring your full, undivided attention to this practice as you listen to the CD or read the following meditation, pausing after each paragraph, and taking enough time to absorb the practice for forty-five, thirty, or fifteen minutes. We recommend practicing the full forty-five minutes (track 11) or thirty minutes (track 10). However, if you're short on time, there is a fifteen-minute practice on the CD (track 9).

Begin your practice by congratulating yourself that you're dedicating some precious time to meditation. May you know that this is an act of love.

As you begin to stop and become present, become aware of the body and mind and whatever is being carried within you—perhaps feelings or thoughts from the day's events or whatever has been going on within you recently.

Simply allow and acknowledge whatever is within and just let it be, without any form of analysis or evaluation.

Gradually, shift the focus of awareness to the breath, breathing normally and naturally. As you breathe in, be aware of breathing in, and as you breathe out, be aware of breathing out.

Just being aware of breathing and focusing awareness on either the tip of the nose or the abdomen. If focusing on the tip of the nose, feel the touch of the air as you breathe in and out. If focusing on the abdomen, feel the belly expanding with each inhalation and contracting with each exhalation.

Just live life one inhalation and one exhalation at a time. Breathing in, breathing out, watching each breath appear and disappear. Just breathing.

Now gently withdraw awareness from the breath and bring it into the world of sensations in the body. Observing without any aversion or indulgence, just acknowledge the multitude of varying sensations as they change from moment to moment and let them be.

As you sense into the body, you may find areas of tension and tightness. If you can allow them to soften and relax, that's fine. If not, just let it be.

If you're unable to soften and relax, acknowledge any persisting sensations and give them space to do whatever they need to do. Simply allow these waves of sensations to flow wherever they need to go.

Now release awareness of sensations and bring attention to hearing, observing all sounds without aversion or indulgence. Be aware of sound at its most basic, fundamental level—simply sound waves that your body is receiving with its faculty of hearing.

Being aware of sounds at this level, just acknowledge the multitude of varying sounds, external and internal, moment to moment.

Whether the sounds are external or internal, just notice how they are ever-changing, revealing the mark of impermanence. Sounds rise, sounds fall. Hear them appear and disappear, just sounds.

Now gently shift attention from awareness of sounds to the mind, to thoughts and emotions. Observe the mind without any aversion or indulgence. Just acknowledge the multitude of varying mental formations moment to moment. Like lying in a field and watching the clouds float by, watch the mind in the same way.

Think of yourself as a meteorologist, just watching internal weather patterns without judgment, just being with the way things are. Thoughts and emotions rise; thoughts and emotions fall. Experiencing them appear and disappear, just thoughts, and just emotions.

You may become aware that the mind has a mind of it own. It analyzes, scrutinizes, plans, and remembers. It catastrophizes, compares, and contrasts. It dreams, blames, and feels sad, angry, and fearful. It fantasizes and has likes and dislikes. The mind is busy thinking about this and that, with thoughts rising, forming, and receding. Experience how they appear and disappear, noticing them as just thoughts.

As you observe and experience your thoughts and emotions, try to avoid falling into them. Rather than getting caught up in the mind's traps, stories, and habits, simply observe them dispassionately, let them be, and know that they will recede in time.

At times you may find yourself caught up in thoughts and feelings, perhaps again and again. When this happens, don't judge or berate yourself. Simply realize that even this awareness is a way of returning to the present moment. Let your awareness recognize that all of these mental states are fleeting and changing, once again revealing impermanence. Once you become aware that your mind has gotten caught up and lost in thoughts and emotions, in that very moment you are no longer caught up. Just continue experiencing the changing nature of mind states. You can consider your mind to be like a white-water river—just thoughts and emotions rolling on and on… If you become frustrated with wandering mind, it's fine to return to the breath for a short time to center yourself.

Very gently now, withdraw awareness from mental events and bring your attention to the present moment itself as the primary object of attention.

Choiceless awareness invites you to become mindful of whatever is arising in the unfolding of each present moment, in the body and in the mind, whether sounds, sensations, or other sensory experiences or a flurry of thoughts or emotions. Just sit back and watch the ever-shifting tides of mind and body. Although you may be sitting very still, your internal experience is quite different. Your body and mind combine to form a dynamic organism interacting with stimuli from the senses and the mind, stimuli that constantly changing.

Simply observe whatever is predominant or compelling in the mind and body and be present to it. If nothing is particularly prevalent and you're unsure of where to focus attention, you can always go back to the breath or any other object as a way to anchor into the here and now.

This practice is analogous to sitting by the edge of a river, just watching whatever goes downstream. Sometimes there are sounds, sometimes sensations, sometimes thoughts and emotions. If nothing much is occurring, you can always come back to the anchor of the breath. Sit and witness the sea of change in your mind and body.

As you learn to give space to whatever is arising inside with greater equanimity and balance, you can begin to go with the flow. Instead of fighting or resisting what's there, you'll come to understand and deeply know that all things change.

Even if you're experiencing storms of anxiety, pain, sadness, anger, or confusion, or perhaps especially at these times, you will know that by giving these feelings space, they will gradually diminish.

Now withdraw from choiceless awareness and come back to the breath, feeling the whole body as you breathe in and out. Feel the entire body rising upward on an inhalation and falling downward on an exhalation. Feel the body as a single, complete organism, connected and whole.

May you again congratulate yourself for practicing this meditation and know that it is contributing to your health and well-being. May you know that this is an act of love.

Sitting Meditation Journal

Take some time to write about whatever came up for you mentally, emotionally, and physically when doing this practice for the first time.

_____

_____

_____

_____

_____

_____

_____

_____

 ## Bob's Story: Rooster Meditation

In the early 1980s I lived at a Buddhist monastery, along with many other monks and a group of six roosters. Having grown up in the city, I assumed that roosters just crow in the morning, at sunrise. It took no time whatsoever to discover that these roosters crowed almost twenty-four hours a day.

On Saturdays we held daylong meditations. The meditation hall was on the first floor, and the roosters often hopped up onto the windowsill to cock-a-doodle-doo all day long. In no time at all, this put me in a state of profound anger. As I wondered why they wouldn't stop cock-a-

doodle-do-ing, I dreamt up many ways to kill a rooster. I could sit on it, shoot it, poison it, burn it, cut it, drown it—my creativity was boundless.

Finally, one day I complained to my teacher, Hlaing Tet Sayadaw, who scolded me and said, "You know nothing about meditation. These roosters are here to teach you. Hearing, hearing, hearing, anger, anger, anger. Go sit back down and practice!"

As time went on, the crowing of the roosters gradually transformed into sound waves— nothing more than audio signals rising and falling. Of course this practice isn't easy, and to this day I can still be provoked at times by the roosters that show up in life—real and metaphorical. But as one's practice slowly grows, patience and understanding will supersede annoyances.

Just Do It!

Stop right now and listen to whatever sounds are in your environment—perhaps a siren, people talking, crickets chirping, or music playing. Notice how the mind is quick to categorize or create an image for each sound, then come back to noticing sounds as just sounds, and their impermanent nature as they come and go. What is it like to listen to sounds without evaluation? Bring this practice with you into your daily life, setting up some sort of reminder so that you'll take time to stop and listen to sounds as just sounds, without judgment.

yoga and mindfulness

It's been said that yoga was developed thousands of years ago in India by meditators who mostly lived in rural areas. Many of them wanted to devote most of their time to sitting meditation practice, yet after many hours of sitting still in one place they often experienced deep aches and pains and could hardly keep their minds still. Because they lived close to animals, the meditators began noticing how various animals stretched and seemed to benefit from it. As time went on, the meditators began copying the animals and soon noticed that their bodies were getting more flexible and stronger. They also discovered that they could sit and meditate for longer periods without discomfort, and that their minds became quieter and still as well. These are the humble origins of yoga, and even today a majority of yoga poses have animal names.

Now that you've begun to practice sitting meditation, you too may feel that you need to stretch and move your body to relieve any aches and pains due to sitting still for extended periods of time. Plus, yoga is an inherently mindful physical practice. In fact, in Sanskrit, *yoga* means "to yoke," in this case bringing together the body and mind. And not only is yoga an excellent way to bring mindfulness to the body in movement, it's also a rejuvenating practice that offers many other health benefits, such as keeping aging bones, joints, muscles, nerves, and organs healthy, supple, and flexible.

formal practice: Mindful Lying Yoga

Mindful yoga involves bringing awareness to your breath, movement, posture, thoughts, and emotions as you practice. You'll need to wear comfortable clothing that doesn't restrict your movements. You'll also need enough space to do the movements, as well as a yoga mat or a carpeted floor. Before you begin, take a look at the following sequence of illustrations so that you can familiarize yourself with the postures in this practice. For ease of practice, listen to the CD, which has three versions of mindful lying yoga practice: fifteen minutes (track 13), thirty minutes (track 14), and forty-five minutes (track 15). Please begin with track 12, which provides an introduction to mindful yoga. Alternatively, you can simply read through the descriptions of the poses below and then practice based on the text. If you haven't been exercising regularly or you aren't very flexible, it's probably best to begin with the fifteen-minute version and work your way up. Listen to your body's wisdom in this regard.

A Word of Caution: Everyone's body is different. Some of us may be more flexible than others. When doing this practice, err on the side of compassionate wisdom. Try to work with these postures slowly and mindfully. And rather than starting at 110 percent, how about just 60 percent at first? It's better to build up your practice slowly than to possibly hurt yourself. Also note that it's wiser to get out of a posture earlier if it's hurting than to stay in it longer and hurt more. If you find yourself unable to do a particular posture, please feel free to skip it. You can consider this a yoga posture too: the posture of not doing a pose and allowing yourself to feel and acknowledge whatever is coming up for you in body and mind. In this light, anything you do or don't do is part of the mindful yoga experience if you bring awareness to it.

Supine Pose

Lie down on your back with your arms by your sides, palms facing up, and breathe naturally for a few breaths.

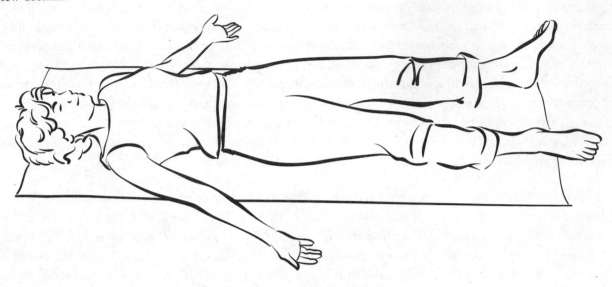

Supine Full Body Stretch

Breathe in and sweep your arms up along the floor, then stretch them overhead with your palms facing each other. Exhale and sweep your arms back down to your sides.

Supine Twist

From this position, sweep your arms out to shoulder height. Bend both knees and raise them straight up, keeping your feet on the floor, then exhale and lower both knees down to your right side, keeping your shoulders and arms on the floor and turning your head to look to the left. Breathe naturally and remain present, being mindful of any waves of sensations, thoughts, or emotions. Inhale and return to the neutral position, lying flat with both knees up and your feet on the floor. Breathe naturally, then repeat on the other side.

Supine Full Body Stretch

Repeat the full body stretch, inhaling and sweeping your arms overhead with palms facing each other, then exhaling as you sweep your arms back down by your sides.

Leg Stretch

Bend your left knee, keeping your left foot on the ground. Keeping your right leg straight, raise it up with your right heel pointing toward the ceiling. Breathe naturally and flex your ankle, pointing your toes toward the ceiling, then rotate your ankle in one direction and then the other. Slowly lower your right leg to the floor. Repeat the full body stretch, then repeat the leg stretch on the other side, bending your right leg and raising your left leg. Once again repeat the full body stretch.

Single Knee to Chest

Keeping your left leg straight, exhale, bend your right knee, and bring it toward your chest, grasping just below the knee with your hands and drawing your thigh closer toward your chest. You can either keep your head on the floor or tuck your chin into your chest. Breathe naturally, being mindful of any waves of sensations, thoughts, or emotions…being present. Slowly return your right foot to the floor and straighten both legs. Repeat on the other side, keeping your right leg straight and drawing your left knee toward your chest. Then once again repeat the full body stretch.

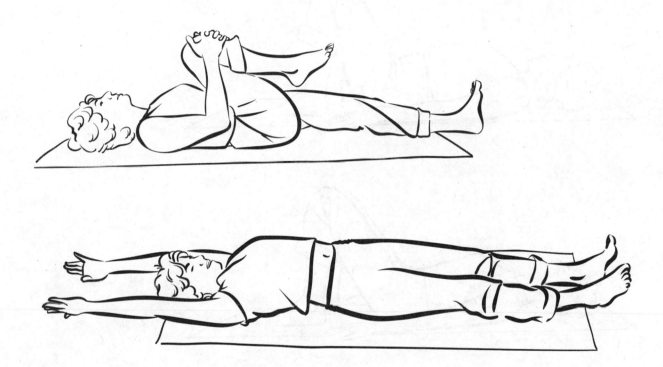

Pelvic Rock and Tilt

Bend both knees and raise them straight up, keeping your feet on the floor. Inhale and press down slightly on your tailbone, allowing your low back to arch gently so that you feel a small gap between your lower back and the floor. Exhale and gently press your lower back down, flush with the floor. Repeat with each breath, rocking and tilting back and forth, being mindful of any waves of sensations, thoughts, or emotions…being present. Repeat the full body stretch.

Bridge Pose

Bend both knees and raise them straight up, keeping your feet on the floor and your arms by your sides. Inhale and curl your spine up off of the floor, lifting first your buttocks, then your lower back, and then your upper back off the floor. Clasp your hands together underneath your body and stretch them toward your feet, breathing naturally. Exhale, return your arms to the starting position, and slowly lower your back down to the floor, one vertebra at a time, like a string of pearls being lowered one at a time, being mindful of any waves of sensations, thoughts, or emotions…being present.

Bridge Pose with Arm Stretch

Repeat the bridge pose, and as you inhale and curl your spine up off the floor, sweep your arms overhead on the floor. As you exhale and lower your back to the floor, sweep your arms back down by your sides. Repeat five times.

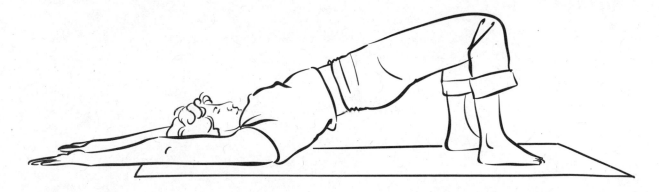

Bridge Pose

Repeat the basic bridge pose, inhaling, curling your spine up off the floor, clasping your hands together underneath your body, and stretching them toward your feet. Then exhale, return your arms to the starting position, and lower your back down to the floor, one vertebra at a time.

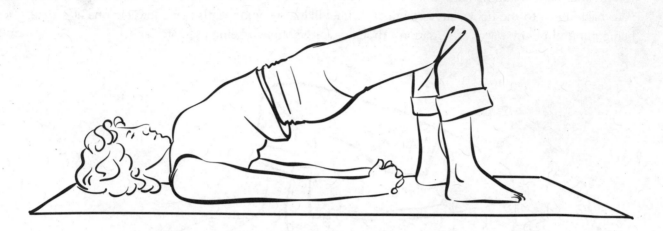

Rocking Back and Forth

Lift up your knees toward your chest, grasp your legs just below the knees, and gently rock back and forth. This is a beautiful counterpose, rocking back and forth and breathing in and out. After rocking in this position several times, keep your thighs to your torso and extend your feet toward the ceiling. Allow your legs to separate and your thighs to drop a bit, alongside your ribs on either side, and gently grasp your feet. Breathe naturally and once again rock back and forth. Then return to the first position, once again grasping just below your knees and rocking back and forth.

Leg Side Stretch

Roll onto your right side with your legs extended, one on top of the other. Let your head rest on your right arm and place your left hand on the floor in front of your ribs. Breathe naturally, then inhale and slowly raise your left leg up, then exhale and slowly lower it back down, being mindful of any waves of sensations, thoughts, or emotions…being present. Repeat a few times, then roll onto your back, draw your knees to your chest, grasp your legs just below the knees and gently rock back and forth once again, breathing in and out. Repeat on the other side.

Prone Leg Stretch

Roll onto your belly and place your hands by your sides. Make fists and place them under your pubic bone for support, then lift both legs until your feet are about six inches off the ground. Breathe in and out, then release and gently lower both legs down to the floor. Place your hands on the floor by each shoulder, with your forearms resting on the floor.

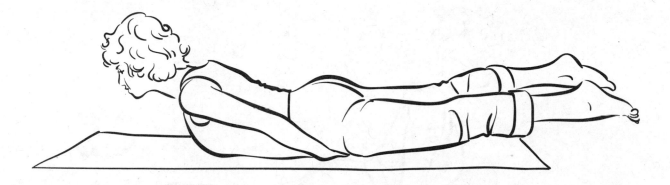

Modified Cobra

Exhale and raise your upper body, supporting the weight of your upper body on your forearms and keeping your waist and legs on the floor. This is a modified cobra pose. Breathe in and out and then release and slowly lower your upper body to the floor with your hands and arms in the same position.

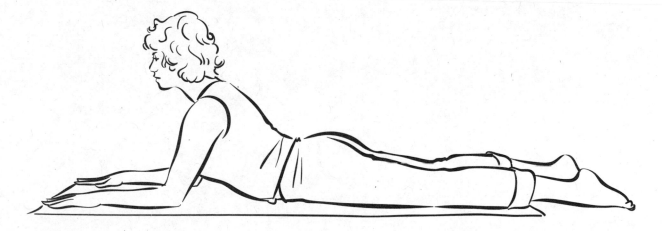

Full Cobra

Repeat the modified cobra, exhaling and raising your upper body, but this time come all the way up onto your hands while still keeping your waist and legs on the floor. This is the full cobra pose. Breathe in and out, being mindful of any waves of sensations, thoughts, or emotions...being present. Inhale and slowly lower your upper body to the floor.

Cow Pose and Cat Pose

Come up on your hands and knees with your arms straight and your hands positioned below your shoulders. Inhale, let your belly sag toward the floor, and lift your head up. This is the cow pose. Exhale and round your back, curling your tailbone toward the floor in a posture like a hissing cat. (Needless to say, this is the cat pose.) Repeat a few times, inhaling into the cow pose and exhaling to the cat pose.

Child's Pose

Lower your torso down to the floor, resting your buttocks on top of your feet, and your head on the floor or on your hands. You may extend your arms in front of you on the floor or place them by your sides on the floor. Breathe naturally.

Bird Dog Pose

Come back up on your hands and knees with your arms straight and your hands positioned below your shoulders. Extend your left leg out behind you level with your hips while extending your right arm out in front of you at shoulder height. Breathe naturally and be mindful of any waves of sensations, thoughts, or emotions...being present. Return to the neutral all-fours position, then repeat on the other side, extending your right leg and left arm.

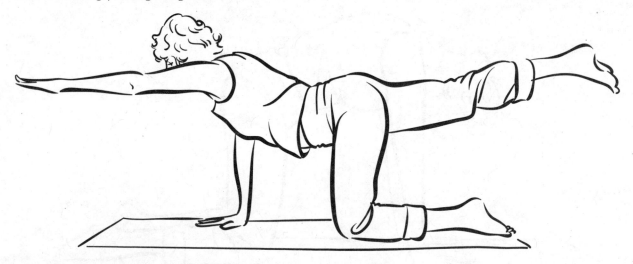

Supine Full Body Pose and Stretch

Lie on your back with your arms by your sides, palms facing up toward the sky, and breathe naturally for a few breaths. Breathe in and sweep your arms up along the floor, then stretch them overhead with your palms facing each other. Exhale and sweep your arms back down to your sides.

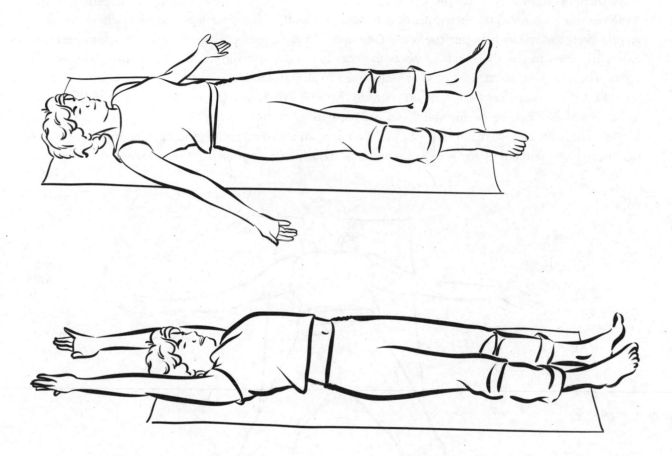

Pose of Openness

Repeat the full body stretch once again, extending your arms overhead as you inhale. When you bring them back down, leave them out at about shoulder height and allow them to gently relax and open as you exhale. Take a moment to feel your arms and armpits being open and to wiggle your fingers and leave them open. Breathe naturally, opening your eyes, mouth, and nostrils, feeling them opening. Bring awareness to your ears and their openness to sounds. Gently relax your legs and allow them to open, feeling even the spaces between the toes being open. Deepen your openness to this pose of openness, extending even to the thousands of pores in your skin and becoming aware of how they, too, are all open. This is a very courageous pose of being open to all possibilities.

Rest here and reflect for a time on your life. Are you living the life you want to be living? Can you feel into whatever may be closing you down and preventing you from living fully? Can you be open to following your heart or your dream for your life? Breathing in and out, resting and opening into the pose of openness, being mindful of any waves of sensations, thoughts, or emotions…being present.

Corpse Pose

Now bring your arms by your sides or place your hands on your chest—whatever is comfortable. Close your eyes and breathe naturally. This final pose is the corpse pose, the pose of deep relaxation. Just as we move in yoga, it is also important to stop and be still. This is the time to assimilate and integrate the movements of your mindful yoga practice. Just as sunlight is crucial to the growth of plants, so too is the darkness of the night. Dormancy and growth work hand in hand to create balance, and so too do motion and stillness. Breathing in and out, may we all be free and at peace, resting in the grace of this universe. May all beings be safe and at peace.

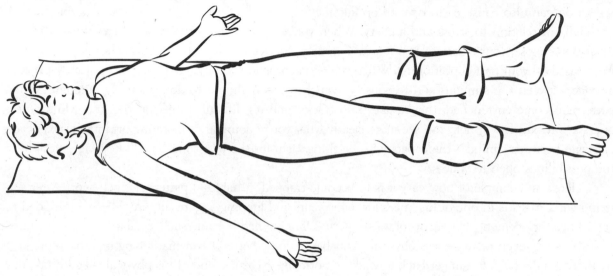

Mindful Lying Yoga Journal

After doing this practice for the first time, take a few moments to write about your experience. What did you notice mentally, emotionally, and physically?

_____

_____

_____

_____

_____

_____

_____

habitual patterns

As you practice sitting meditation, you'll become increasingly aware of not only the physical sensations within you and other sensory stimuli, but also your thoughts and emotions. This is among the most important reasons for practicing mindfulness: It allows you to learn about what's going on "under the hood" to fuel and drive your behaviors. This is especially beneficial when it allows you to observe patterns of living that don't necessarily serve your health and well-being or the quality of your relationships.

Human beings are often creatures of habit, and this isn't always necessarily a bad thing. Habits help us get daily tasks done smoothly and efficiently without forethought or afterthought. But day-to-day repetition can also cause us to operate on automatic pilot, which can definitely be counterproductive, especially in relation to stress and anxiety. When you're operating on autopilot, you're unlikely to see, much less choose, your reactions to stress and anxiety. As a result, you may impulsively react in habitual ways based on your past conditioning. When you're on autopilot, you may not even recognize that there's a space between the stimulus and response in which you can choose to do something different. When patterns become entrenched, they're like train tracks, and it's difficult to get off the line. Mindfulness offers a way out. It will help you see more clearly what you're doing and, more importantly, *why*. As you cultivate beginner's mind—the capacity to see things as if for the first time—you'll be aware of more of the possibilities open to you.

Here's an example of how easy it is to become trapped in habitual patterns of behavior: After suffering with arthritis in one of his knees for many years and limping as a result, an older man decided to get a knee replacement. His recovery was slow, and limping had become such a habit that he continued to walk poorly even once he was physically capable of doing better. Over many long months, a physical therapist finally helped him get back to walking normally. Near the end of his physical therapy, one day the appointment ended right before noon, and few minutes after the patient left, the physical therapist went out to get lunch. Out on the street, she noticed the patient walking with another person but once again limping. Dumbfounded, she approached the patient and asked him what was going on. He replied, "I'm just walking with my cousin like I always do."

Sadly, we often create our own limitations through incorrect assumptions and habitual behaviors. Without mindfulness, we can be like cows in a corral with an electric fence. At first the cows bump up against the fence and get shocked, but soon they learn to avoid it. At that point, you can shut off the electricity and the cows still won't approach the fence again. Freedom is close at hand, since they could easily knock down the fence and escape, but the cows are now confined by their own minds. Does this sound familiar?

Such is the nature of habitual patterns and fear of change. It's a sad fact that many dysfunctional relationships continue because fear of the unknown is greater than the difficulty or heartache of continuing with something familiar but problematic. In many cases, we would rather suffer with what we know than face the unknown. The challenge is to expand our perceptions and horizons and be curious about what sets off our triggers and reactions.

resilience and stress

Why is it that some people view adversity as a challenge and imbue it with meaning while others perceive it with trepidation and fear? One key characteristic in this regard is resilience, which helps people see things differently and respond more skillfully.

Several decades ago, researcher and psychologist Suzanne Kobasa found that stress-hardy individuals showed higher levels of control and commitment and willingness to rise to a challenge (Kabat-Zinn 1990). In this context, control refers to the belief that you can have an effect on your stress and anxiety, and commitment means that you're willing to give it your best and endure most hardships. Viewing adversity as a challenge means that you welcome even difficult situations, viewing them as an opportunity to learn and grow. Similarly, Israeli medical sociologist Aaron Antonovsky studied people who had survived extreme stress and discovered that they had what he called an inherent sense of coherence about the world and themselves (Kabat-Zinn 1990). This sense of coherence is characterized by the ability to view challenges as something that can be understood and managed, and that can offer valuable lessons.

A concrete example is a friend named Frank, who contracted polio when he was young and spent a couple of years in an iron lung. The disease left him almost a complete quadriplegic, able to move only his right foot. Rather than shrinking from the challenge of living a full life, Frank learned to drive a specially equipped van with just his right foot, got a college education in computer science, and is able to do his job by typing with a mouth stick. Frank faces challenges every day, since he can't unzip his zipper, feed himself, clothe himself, or even scratch an itch. Every night he has to be put on a respirator to breathe while he sleeps. He says that taking care of him is like taking care of a baby, yet he still has a tremendously positive attitude about life. When asked how he got to be so resilient, he said, "I decided early on that it wasn't worth my time to worry—that it's totally unproductive. I chose to look on the good side of things."

Frank has many of the traits that Dr. Kobasa and Dr. Antonovsky associate with stress hardiness. He lives with a deep sense of coherence despite the considerable challenges and hardships he faces. Frank is an inspiration, showing us that even the greatest adversity can be seen as a challenge to overcome. Taking steps into the unknown can be frightening, but who knows what you may discover and how you might benefit or grow from what you learn? If you hold back from life, you may miss out on many things.

Use your mindfulness practice to become aware of old patterns that really don't serve your health and well-being. As you grow in your capacity to see things with beginner's mind, you'll open to new possibilities and discover new pathways to greater freedom. In her wonderful poem "Autobiography in Five Short Chapters," Portia Nelson describes the way we sometimes get stuck, and then points the way to greater awareness and freedom:

Chapter One
I walk down the street.
> There is a deep hole in the sidewalk.
> I fall in.
> I am lost…I am helpless.
>> It isn't my fault…
It takes forever to find a way out.

Chapter Two
I walk down the same street.
> There is a deep hole in the sidewalk.
> I pretend I don't see it.
> I fall in again.
I can't believe I am in this same place.
>> But, it isn't my fault.
It still takes a long time to get out.

Chapter Three
I walk down the same street.
> There is a deep hole in the sidewalk.
> I *see* it is there.
> I still fall…it's a habit…but,
>> my eyes are open.
>> I know where I am.
It is *my* fault.
I get out immediately.

Chapter Four
I walk down the same street.
> There is a deep hole in the sidewalk.
> I walk around it.

Chapter Five
I walk down another street.

> —Portia Nelson, "Autobiography in Five Short Chapters" (1994, 2-3)

explore: Understanding Your Habitual Patterns

Spend a little time reflecting on any of your own habitual patterns that may be a result of anxiety. For example do you say things you wish you hadn't because you're anxious? Do you eat or not eat when you're anxious? Do you repeat certain actions or other patterns over and over to get temporary relief from obsessive thoughts or a racing mind? Take a moment to explore any habitual patterns that come to mind. If you're at a loss, think of people, food, or work.

_____

_____

_____

_____

_____

_____

_____

Based on what you wrote in response to the previous question, do you engage in certain habitual behaviors that might be adding to your stress and anxiety? For example, maybe you stay up too late and don't get a good night's sleep. Maybe you eat unhealthy fast food to save time and money or go out to eat too often. Perhaps you spend too much money or spend too much time at work, at the expense of your health and well-being. Take a moment to list any habitual behaviors that might be adding to your stress, anxiety, or other difficulties in life.

_____

_____

_____

_____

_____

_____

_____

Most of us are creatures of habit. Some habits can be very helpful, like exercising regularly or eating healthfully, and some aren't helpful, like working too much and not sleeping enough. Most of us have just this sort of combination of habits—some healthful and others that diminish our well-being and quality of life. Bringing mindfulness to how you do things can help you more clearly see your habitual patterns so that you can make changes.

Before you move on, take a few moments to connect with your breath and mindfully reflect on what you just wrote, compassionately acknowledging, validating, and integrating what you learned from this exploration.

informal practice: Being Mindful of Habits

You just spent some time reflecting on and writing about some of your habitual patterns. Over the next week, make it an informal practice to be mindful of your habits, both those that serve your health and well-being and those that don't. Notice what happens when you become mindful of them. Can you see that once you're mindful of a habit or that you're about to engage in it, you have more choice in how to respond?

 Planning and Reviewing Your Practice

Here are the formal practices from this chapter. Go ahead and put them on your calendar over the next week. Try to practice at least five days a week. You can either alternate the practices from day to day, or you might combine them, starting with mindful lying yoga and continuing with sitting meditation. Also schedule a time about a week from now when you'll review your practice to see how it's going.

Formal Practices

- ☐ Sitting Meditation

- ☐ Mindful Lying Yoga

Now you have six informal practices to integrate into your daily life.

Informal Practices

- ☐ Being Mindful of Habits

- ☐ Minding Your Pain

- ☐ STOP

- ☐ Bringing the Eight Attitudes of Mindfulness into Your Life

- ☐ Weaving Mindfulness Throughout Your Day

- ☐ Mindful Eating

Formal Practice Log

Each time you do a formal practice, fill out the following log. As you fill it out, and as you look back over the previous week's practice, think about how your practice has been going. Do you notice any patterns about what works best for you? What changes could you make to sustain the discipline?

Date and practice	Time	Thoughts, feelings, and sensations that arose during this practice and how you felt afterward

Reflecting on Informal Practice

Take some time every day to reflect on at least one instance of informal practice. You can use what you learn from these reflections to deepen your daily informal practice.

Practice	What was the situation?	What did you notice before?	What did you notice after?	What did you learn?

meditation for anxiety and stress

As you've been working your way through this book, you've learned quite a bit about the stress reaction, its ill effects on well-being, and how mindfulness can help. You've done some exploration of your own stressors and how they affect your life, as well as habitual patterns that may be exacerbating your stress or anxiety. Hopefully this information and exploration has motivated you to devote time to the practices you've learned so far—both informal practices that you can weave into your day-to-day life and the formal practices we've guided you through, such as the mindful check-in, mindful breathing, the body scan, and seated mindfulness meditation. Now you're ready to integrate all of this information, exploration, and practice in a meditation designed specifically for working with anxiety and stress. This practice combines mindful breathing, the body scan, and mindfulness of thoughts with a new practice: mindful self-inquiry. While all of the explorations and practices in this book will help you develop mindfulness and better cope with stress, adding self-inquiry to the mix will make your practice more effective by focusing in on the issues and situations most relevant to your life and your stress.

mindful self-inquiry

Mindful self-inquiry is an investigation into the nature of one's own mind and being. In the context of this book, that inquiry looks into physical sensations, emotions, and thoughts that may be contributing to stress and anxiety. In your daily life, you may be so busy doing that you feel you have little or no time for self-reflection. Yet this exploration is extremely worthwhile, as fears often lie beneath the surface of awareness.

When you practice mindful self-inquiry, you bring kind awareness and acknowledgment to any stressed or anxious feelings in the body and mind and simply allow them to be. This means staying with those feelings without analyzing, suppressing, or encouraging them. Although this may seem scary in and of itself, realize that when you allow yourself to feel and acknowledge your worries, irritations, painful memories, and other difficult thoughts and emotions, this often helps them dissipate. By going with what's happening rather than expending energy fighting or turning away from it, you create the opportunity to gain insight into what's driving your concerns. When you begin to understand the underlying causes of your apprehension, freedom and a sense of spaciousness naturally emerge. In essence, this is a process of learning to trust and stay with feelings of discomfort rather than trying to escape from or analyze them. This often leads to a remarkable shift; time and again your feelings will show you everything you need to know about them—and something you need to know for your own well-being.

informal practice: RAIN

A little later in this chapter, we'll guide you through a meditation for self-inquiry into stress and anxiety. In the meantime, you can use the acronym RAIN as an informal practice for working with mindful self-inquiry:

R = Recognize when a strong emotion is present.

A = Allow or acknowledge that it's there.

I = Investigate the body, emotions, and thoughts.

N = Non-identify with whatever is there.

RAIN is an insightful self-inquiry practice that you can bring into your daily life to help you discover deeper threads of what triggers strong emotional reactions. Throughout the next week, bring recognition to any strong emotion and allow it to be present. Investigate what you feel physically, mentally, and emotionally and see where it takes you. The last element, non-identification, is very useful because it helps to deflate the mind's stories and cultivates the understanding that strong emotions are just another passing mind state and not a definition of who you are. It's like going to a movie, where you sit back and watch the actors play out the drama. By seeing your story as impermanent and not identifying with it, you'll begin to loosen the grip of your own mind traps. This will help create the space for you to be with things as they are and deepen your understanding of what drives, underlies, or fuels your fears, anger, and sadness. It also grants you the freedom to look at the situation differently and choose a response other than what may be dictated by your story.

Turning Into Emotions

Turning into difficult emotions can feel a bit foreign, since our culture so often emphasizes suppressing, denying, or eradicating pain. Isn't it time to start acknowledging these parts of ourselves rather than continuing to avoid or ignore them? If we learn to view these challenges as rites of passage instead of running away from them, we'll gain the opportunity to learn and grow, and perhaps even change the circumstances that lead to distress.

Have you ever wondered why it's called "life insurance" when it's really death insurance? Have you ever wondered why it's called "health insurance" when it's really sickness insurance? These questions may sound silly, but they serve as a reminder of how pervasively the media and our culture shift the focus from difficult topics. We're surrounded by messages indicating that we should stay young, have a great body, and turn to medications anytime we're sick, sad, or scared. While taking medication can at times be vital for health and well-being, it's also important to cultivate inner resilience in dealing with stress, pain, and even illness.

Turning into difficult emotions and facing stress, anxiety, or pain isn't an easy path. It may seem unsafe, and you may have to overcome a feeling of unwillingness. But what else is there to do? As the saying goes, "You can run, but you can't hide." You're likely to find that when you don't deal with your pain, it gets larger, and eventually it may get too heavy to carry any further. In a collection of aphorisms, Franz Kafka said, "You can hold back from suffering of the world, you have free permission to do so and it is in accordance with your nature, but perhaps this very holding back is the one suffering that you could have avoided" (1946, 158).

Bob's Story: A Personal Inquiry

Many years ago, I was on the telephone in my office, talking with a hospital administrator about the mindfulness-based stress reduction program. I felt that she didn't understand one of my concerns and wasn't being supportive of the program. As the conversation went on, I began to feel upset and almost lashed out at her. Fortunately, I looked at my clock and realized I needed to end the call because I had an appointment.

After the appointment I was still upset about the phone call, so I tried to ground myself by bringing awareness to the breath, but my mind immediately wandered back to the phone conversation and got all caught up in the story again. I began to fume, thinking, "When I get done with this meditation, I'm going to call her and let her have it!" Recognizing that I had wandered off, I acknowledged, "Oh, wandering mind," but before I knew it, I was right back there again, getting mad and thinking about how I was going to get retribution. Eventually I realized that I was extremely angry, perhaps beyond what the conversation called for, and needed to investigate this further.

I began my mindful self-inquiry into the anger by simply recognizing and acknowledging that I was indeed very angry. I tried to simply feel into the anger without attempting to figure it out. It was challenging and uncomfortable, and more than once I found myself right back in my reactive story. Eventually, I began to feel another emotion emerging: sadness—a big sadness. I felt into the sadness in the same way, and in time, it opened to a memory of not feeling understood by other hospital administrators while trying to enlighten them about mindfulness. As I stayed with the feeling of not being understood, I began to feel there was more to be revealed. I continued feeling into the pain, and gradually a deeper insight arose. I recognized an old and familiar feeling of not being seen, understood, or accepted by others. As I felt into that, I realized just how much of my life I'd spent trying to get approval or validation from others. It was painful to realize this, but it was also tremendously freeing. Now that I understood what was being triggered, I realized that I didn't need to continue or escalate the "conflict" with the hospital administrator. In fact, when I reflected on our conversation, I realized that she was actually trying to be supportive, but my preconceptions and habitual patterns stood in the way of my seeing that.

Finding Your Heart

In mindful self-inquiry, you learn to acknowledge and investigate any feelings you'd like to know more about. Though it may be challenging, turning toward fears and other difficult feelings can reveal hidden jewels. Acknowledging your fears and inquiring into them in this way will open the door to deeper understanding, and with it, compassion and peace. In her poem "Unconditional," Jennifer Paine Welwood eloquently describes this journey and the potential it offers for profound transformation:

> Willing to experience aloneness,
> I discover connection everywhere;
> Turning to face my fear,
> I meet the warrior who lives within;
> Opening to my loss,
> I gain the embrace of the universe;
> Surrendering into emptiness,
> I find fullness without end.
> Each condition I flee from pursues me,
> Each condition I welcome transforms me,
> And becomes itself transformed
> Into its radiant jewel-like essence.
> I bow to the one who has made it so,
> Who has crafted this Master Game;
> To play it is purest delight—
> To honor its form, true devotion.
>
> —Jennifer Paine Welwood, "Unconditional" (1998, 21)

formal practice: Mindful Self-Inquiry for Stress and Anxiety

You can do mindful self-inquiry either lying down or sitting up, but if you lie down and find yourself falling asleep, try a more upright posture. Bring your full, undivided attention to this practice as you listen to track 16 on the CD or read the meditation below, pausing after each paragraph to fully absorb this practice for thirty minutes.

Begin your practice by congratulating yourself that you're dedicating some precious time to meditation. May you know that this is an act of love.

As you begin to stop and become present, become aware of the body and mind and whatever is being carried within you—perhaps feelings or thoughts from the day's events or whatever has been going on within you recently.

Simply allow and acknowledge whatever is within and just let it be, without any form of analysis or evaluation.

Gradually, shift your focus of awareness to the breath, breathing normally and naturally. As you breathe in, be aware of breathing in, and as you breathe out, be aware of breathing out.

Just being aware of breathing and focusing awareness on the abdomen, feeling the belly expanding with each inhalation and contracting with each exhalation.

Just living life one inhalation and one exhalation at a time. Breathing in, breathing out, watching each breath appear and disappear. Just breathing.

Now gently withdraw attention from the breath and enter into the world of sensations in the body.

Scan through the body part by part. As you do the body scan, feel and acknowledge any sensations. At first, it's important to just feel into sensations since it's so easy to get lost in thoughts. Just ride the waves of sensations moment to moment. You may become aware of thoughts and emotions as well. Simply note them without analysis or judgment, and without getting caught up in them.

And now gently withdraw awareness from the body scan as you shift to mindful inquiry, investigating any emotions, thoughts, or physical sensations that lie beneath the surface of awareness and may be driving anxieties and fears.

Gently direct your attention into any feeling of fear, anxiety, or other difficult emotions. Allow yourself to sense into the emotion, acknowledging what it feels like in the body and mind.

To begin this exploration, you need first to check in with yourself and determine whether it feels safe or not. If you don't feel safe, perhaps it's better to wait and try another time, and for now, just stay with your breathing. Take a moment to check in right now. If you don't feel like continuing with the inquiry that follows, listen to yourself. This may be your wise and compassionate mind and heart speaking. Know that you can continue with the inquiry another time. If you don't feel like continuing, you can now go to breathing meditation.

If you're feeling safe, bring awareness into the body and mind and begin to allow yourself to feel into and acknowledge any physical sensations, emotions, or thoughts, Just letting them be, without trying to analyze them or figure them out.

You may discover that within these feelings lies a whole plethora of thoughts, emotions, or memories that are causing the fear, anxiety, or other difficult emotions. When you begin to acknowledge what hasn't been acknowledged, the doorway into insight and understanding opens. As you turn toward your emotions, they may show you what you're worried, mad, sad, or bewildered about.

You may learn that the resistance to unacknowledged emotions often causes more fear, and that learning to go with them, rather than fighting them, can diminish their power.

Simply go with whatever you feel, in mind and body, allowing and acknowledging whatever you feel. Just letting the waves of emotions, thoughts, and sensations go wherever they need to go.

By acknowledging your fears and other difficult emotions, you may open the door to deeper understanding, compassion, and peace.

Now gently withdraw from mindful inquiry and bring your attention to the mind, to thoughts and emotions. Observe the mind without any aversion or indulgence. Just acknowledge the multitude of varying mental formations moment to moment. Like lying in a field and watching the clouds float by, watch the mind in the same way.

You may become aware that the mind has a mind of it own. It analyzes, scrutinizes, plans, remembers, compares, and contrasts. It dreams, fantasizes, and has likes and dislikes. The mind is busy thinking about this and that, with thoughts rising, forming, and receding. Watch them appear and disappear, noticing them as just thoughts.

Think of yourself as a meteorologist, just watching internal weather patterns without judgment, just being with the way things are. Thoughts rise, thoughts fall. Watch them appear and disappear, just thoughts.

As you learn to give space to whatever is arising inside with greater equanimity and balance, you can begin to go with the flow. Instead of fighting or resisting what's there, you'll come to understand and deeply know that all things change.

Even if you're experiencing storms of anxiety, pain, sadness, anger, or confusion, or perhaps especially at these times, you will know that by giving these feelings space, they will gradually diminish.

Now withdraw from observing mind states, come back to the breath, and feel the whole body as you breathe in and out. Feel the entire body rising upward on an inhalation and falling downward on an exhalation. Feel the body as a single, complete organism, connected and whole.

May you again congratulate yourself for practicing this meditation and know that it is contributing to your health and well-being. May you know that this is an act of love. May all beings be at peace.

Mindful Self-Inquiry for Stress and Anxiety Journal

Take some time to write about whatever came up for you mentally, emotionally, and physically when doing this practice for the first time.

_____

_____

_____

_____

_____

_____

_____

_____

formal practice: Mindful Standing Yoga

As a reminder, mindful yoga involves bringing awareness to your breath, movement, posture, thoughts, and emotions as you practice. Wear comfortable clothing that doesn't restrict your movements and be sure you have enough space to do the movements. We suggest using a yoga mat. Before you begin, take a look at the following sequence of illustrations so that you can familiarize yourself with the postures in this practice. For ease of practice, listen to the CD, which has three versions of mindful standing yoga practice: fifteen minutes (track 17), thirty minutes (track 18), and forty-five minutes (track 19). Please begin with track 12, as a refresher on the basics of mindful yoga. Alternatively, you can simply read through the descriptions of the poses below and then practice based on the text. If you haven't been exercising regularly or you aren't very flexible, it's probably best to begin with the fifteen-minute version and work your way up. Listen to your body's wisdom in this regard. In any case, please review the words of caution in the lying yoga exercise in the previous chapter, so that you practice with wisdom and compassion for your body.

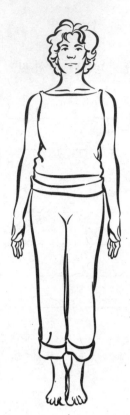

Mountain Pose

Stand upright with your arms by your sides and palms slightly open. Don't lean forward or backward, and keep your head squarely between your shoulders. Distribute your weight evenly between both feet and keep your knees, hips, and shoulders aligned. Breathe naturally.

Standing Full Body Stretch

Inhale and raise both arms out to your sides and then up overhead with your palms facing each other. Gaze straight out and stretch your arms and torso up, toward the sky. Exhale and slowly lower your arms back to your sides with awareness. Breathe in and out, then repeat two more times.

Horizontal Arm Stretch

Inhale and raise both arms up to shoulder level with your arms extended and palms facing upward; alternatively, you can start with palms facing down and flex your wrists so that your palms face straight out, away from you. Exhale and slowly lower your arms back to your sides with awareness. Breathe in and out, then repeat two more times.

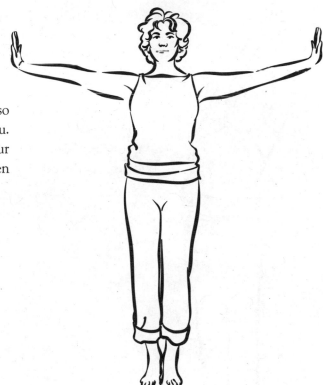

One-Arm Stretch

Breathing naturally, bring your right arm up overhead, stretching towards the sky, as you simultaneously lift your left heel, keeping the toes of your left foot on the ground. Slowly release and return to the mountain pose, then repeat on the other side.

Side-Bending Stretch

Inhale and raise both arms up overhead. Lock your thumbs together and exhale. Inhale, standing tall and stretching upward, then exhale and, keeping your torso facing forward, bend to the right side, breathing in and out and being mindful of any waves of sensations, thoughts, or emotions... being present. Return to an upright position, with your arms stretched up toward the sky, then exhale and slowly lower your arms to your sides. Repeat on the other side.

Shoulder Rolls

Standing in the mountain pose, raise and lower your shoulders with awareness, circling them first forward, then backward, and then returning to a neutral position.

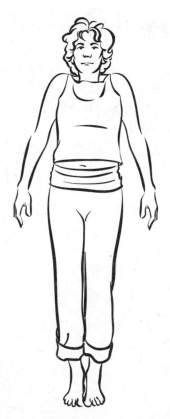

Neck Stretch

Slowly bring your right ear toward your right shoulder without lifting the shoulder up. Breathe naturally. Repeat on the other side.

Diagonal Neck Stretch

Bring your right ear toward your right shoulder without lifting the shoulder up. Keeping your right arm by your side, open the palm of your right hand and face it forward. Drop and turn your head to look at the palm of your right hand, stretching your neck diagonally. Breathe naturally. Return to the starting position, then repeat on the other side. Return to the mountain pose.

Standing Full Body Stretch

Repeat the full body stretch, inhaling and raising both arms up overhead, then exhaling and slowly lowering your arms back to your sides with awareness. Breathe in and out, then repeat two more times.

Standing Twist I

Place your hands on your hips, inhale, and stand up tall. Exhale and, keeping your hips facing forward, twist your torso to the right and look over your right shoulder, being mindful of any waves of sensations, thoughts, or emotions…being present. Breathe naturally, then release and return to the starting position. Repeat on the other side.

Standing Twist II

Repeat the standing twist on both sides, this time allowing your hips and legs to rotate and keeping just your feet stationary and pointing forward. Release and return to the mountain pose.

Center Field Position

Gently bend your knees and bend slightly forward, placing your hands on your thighs. Breathe naturally. Maintaining the position of your legs and upper body, lift your arms up overhead in line with your spine, with your palms facing each other. Breathe naturally, then return to the mountain pose.

Forward Bend

Inhale and raise your arms up overhead in a full body stretch, then exhale and slowly bring your hands down toward the floor. Stop when you need to inhale, rest for a breath, and then exhale and stretch further down. You may slightly bend your knees. When you're down as far as you can comfortably go, breathe naturally for a few breaths. Inhale and slowly return to the starting position, pausing as you exhale and then returning to the mountain pose. Repeat three times.

Standing Full Body Stretch

Repeat the full body stretch, inhaling and raising both arms up overhead, then exhaling and slowly lowering your arms back to your sides with awareness. Breathe in and out, then repeat two more times.

Balance Pose I

For this pose, feel free to hold on to something until you develop better balance. Beginning in the mountain pose, feel your body balanced evenly on both feet, with your knees, hips, and shoulders aligned. Feeling your left foot solidly on the ground, bend your right knee and raise it in front of you as high as you comfortably can while maintaining your balance. Breathe naturally, being mindful of any waves of sensations, thoughts, or emotions...being present. Release and repeat on the other side. As you develop better balance, you can raise the knee higher and extend your arms overhead.

Modified Triangle

Starting in the mountain pose, rotate your right foot out with the heel at the center of your left foot, forming a T. Take a wide step out to the side with your right leg and balance yourself in this position, with your weight evenly distributed between your feet. Breathe naturally. Bend your right knee and right elbow and bend over to your right side, placing your right forearm on your right thigh. Extend your left arm overhead, by your left ear, and breathe naturally. Feel the symmetry from the outstretched arm overhead aligned with your straight leg. Reverse the motion to return to the mountain pose, then repeat on the other side.

Full Triangle

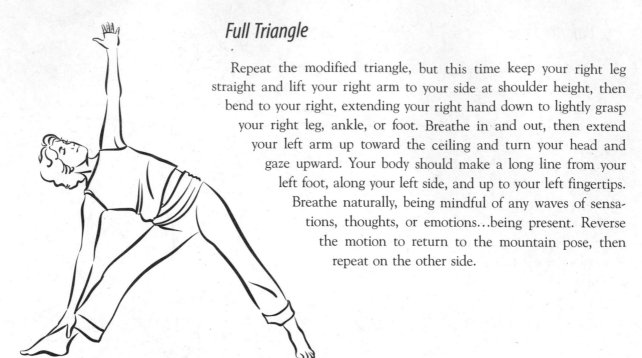

Repeat the modified triangle, but this time keep your right leg straight and lift your right arm to your side at shoulder height, then bend to your right, extending your right hand down to lightly grasp your right leg, ankle, or foot. Breathe in and out, then extend your left arm up toward the ceiling and turn your head and gaze upward. Your body should make a long line from your left foot, along your left side, and up to your left fingertips. Breathe naturally, being mindful of any waves of sensations, thoughts, or emotions…being present. Reverse the motion to return to the mountain pose, then repeat on the other side.

Balance Pose II

For this pose, feel free to hold on to something until you develop better balance. Beginning in the mountain pose, feel your body balanced evenly on both feet, with your knees, hips, and shoulders aligned. Feeling your left foot solidly on the ground, bend your right knee and lift your right foot up behind you. Grasp your right ankle or pant cuff with your right hand and draw the heel a little closer to your buttocks if you can. Raise your left arm up toward the ceiling and breathe naturally. Release and breathe mindfully for a few breaths, then repeat on the other side.

Warrior Pose

Starting in the mountain pose, rotate your right foot out with the heel at the center of your left foot, forming a T. Take a wide step out to the side with your right leg and balance yourself in this position, with your weight evenly distributed between your feet. Breathe naturally. Extend your arms from your sides at shoulder level, then bend your right knee, aligning it over your right ankle, and gaze out beyond your right arm, keeping your torso stationary. Breathe naturally, then gently release and return to the mountain pose. Breathe naturally for a few breaths, then repeat on the other side, again returning to the mountain pose for a few breaths.

Standing Full Body Stretch

Repeat the full body stretch, inhaling and raising both arms up overhead, then exhaling and slowly lowering your arms back to your sides with awareness. Breathe in and out, then repeat two more times.

Downward-Facing Dog

Bend your knees and place your hands on the floor so that your knees are under your hips and your hands are under your shoulders. Inhale and lift your hips and buttocks up to form an inverted V or U shape. This pose is strenuous, so approach it gently and breathe naturally. Initially, you may need to keep your knees slightly bent. To increase your flexibility, alternately bring one heel down and then the other to stretch your legs. As you gain flexibility, try bringing both heels down to the floor. Release and return to the mountain pose.

Standing Full Body Stretch

Repeat the full body stretch, inhaling and raising both arms up overhead, then exhaling and slowly lowering your arms back to your sides with awareness. Breathe in and out, then repeat two more times.

Sitting Stretch

Gently make a transition to sitting on the floor with both feet extended straight out in front of you. Sit upright, lift your chest, and breathe naturally. Gently release.

Groin Stretch

From this seated position, bend your knees and bring the soles of your feet together, letting your knees fall out to the sides. Slowly draw your feet toward your body, keeping them centered and bringing them as close to your groin as you comfortably can, either by grasping your feet and pulling them toward your groin, or by placing your hands on the floor behind you and inching your body forward, toward your feet. Breathe naturally, being mindful of any waves of sensations, thoughts, or emotions... being present.

Forward Bend

While still in the groin stretch, release your right leg and extend it straight out in front of you on the floor, tucking your left foot further into your groin if possible. Inhale and extend your arms up toward the ceiling with your palms facing each other. Exhale and bend forward, extending your arms in front of you and grasping your right leg, ankle, or foot. If you are straining, be gentle with yourself. You're welcome to either bend your knee or place a pillow underneath it to do this stretch. Breathe naturally. Release the posture, returning to an upright seated position, then extend your left leg straight out in front of you and tuck your right foot into your groin. Repeat the forward bend, this time grasping your left leg, ankle, or foot. Release and return to an upright seated position with both legs extended in front of you.

Seated Twist

Keeping your left foot on the floor, bend your left leg, raising your knee straight up and drawing your left heel as close to your body as you comfortably can. Inhale and wrap your right elbow around your left knee, placing your left hand on the floor behind your left buttock, then exhale and rotate your torso to the left. Breathe naturally, being mindful of any waves of sensations, thoughts, or emotions…being present. Inhale and return to the starting position, then repeat on the other side.

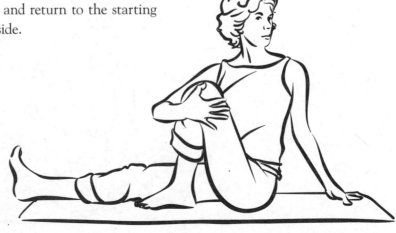

Corpse Pose

Now lie on your back with your arms by your sides or your hands on your chest—whatever is comfortable. Close your eyes and breathe naturally. This final pose is the corpse pose, the pose of deep relaxation. Just as we move in yoga, it is also important to stop and be still. This is the time to assimilate and integrate the movements of your mindful yoga practice. Just as sunlight is crucial to the growth of plants, so too is the darkness of the night. Dormancy and growth work hand in hand to create balance, and so too do motion and stillness. Breathing in and out, may we all be free and at peace, resting in the grace of this universe. May all beings be safe and at peace.

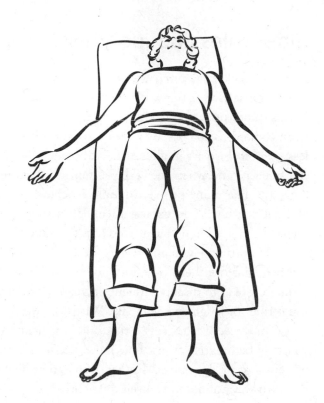

Mindful Standing Yoga Journal

After doing this practice for the first time, take a few moments to write about your experience. What did you notice mentally, emotionally, and physically?

_____

_____

_____

_____

_____

_____

inner rules and judgments

It's remarkable how often we operate from belief systems filled with numerous inner rules about how others, ourselves, or the world *should* be. Just think of the amount of energy you exert trying to change things to be the way you want them to be. Maybe you believe that it's wrong or unfair that others don't work as hard as you do. As a result, you may become resentful and angry. You might also start working less, even if this isn't in alignment with your values. Or maybe you think people shouldn't cut you off on the freeway, and when they do, you tailgate them to show your disapproval, which could cause an accident. Or, like many people, you might believe that your partner should know your feelings and desires without you having to express them. With time, you may become increasingly resentful if your feelings aren't recognized and your wishes aren't honored.

Unfortunately, many things are beyond our control, particularly events in the larger world and the behavior of others. So efforts to change these things often sap our energy for other endeavors and ultimately lead to disappointment, increased anxiety, and even angst. Make it a practice to notice when inner rules or judgments come up. When the word "should" comes into your mind or out of your mouth, check in to see if it reflects a rule or a judgment. As you become mindful of inner rules and "shoulds," you may be amazed at just how much you're driven by them. Again, don't take this as an opportunity to berate or judge yourself. Rather, realize that developing this awareness is the first step in choosing to relate to the world and yourself differently.

FAQ

How do I get myself unstuck from seeing things in a certain way?

Sadly, our limitations are often self-created through our own misperceptions. Awareness will assist you in breaking out of your habitual conditioning. Until you can see where you are and what you're experiencing, you might not be able to make changes. Practicing mindfulness can help you break out of your ordinary patterns and wake you from the slumbers of unawareness. If that sounds too abstract, perhaps this story will help: A combat pilot was on a mission when enemy gunfire punctured his plane's hydraulic fluid reservoir. He was in big trouble, since this meant he couldn't open his landing gear. As he wondered how he was going to get his plane down safely, he started to freak out but then realized his only hope lay in calming his mind. In the silence he discovered an idea. Even though there was no extra hydraulic fluid on the plane, another type of fluid was available. He asked his squadron of soldiers to plug the holes as best they could, then urinate into the hydraulic fluid tank. This was definitely an unconventional approach, but it did allow him to open the landing gear and land the plane safely.

❀ Allison's Story

Allison believed she was the hardest-working person in the human resources department of the large corporation where she worked. Yet she had been there for eighteen months and had never received a raise. She was increasingly plagued by thoughts like "I can't believe they haven't given me a raise. They should know I deserve it." She continued to work hard, but all the while her resentment, frustration, and bitterness were building, and she started getting stomach pains. She became increasingly distracted, and eventually the quality of her work started to slip.

One day while she was out having lunch with a coworker, she couldn't keep her feelings in anymore and said, "It's unbelievable that no one has approached me about a raise. This is a bad situation. Jerry got a raise two months ago, and we started at the same time. It's not fair. Maybe I need to look for a new job."

Her friend replied, "Well, have you asked them for a raise? That's what Jerry did." Dumbfounded, Allison replied, "Ask them for a raise? Why would I do that? They should know how hard I work and that I deserve it. I shouldn't have to ask."

Her friend replied, "Ah, the shoulds. Keep thinking like that, and it's unlikely you'll get a raise anytime soon."

"What do you mean?" Allison asked.

"Well, let's put it this way: Whenever you use "shoulds," you set a rule in your mind and limit your potential or your way of seeing things. Maybe they should know how hard you work, but your manager is a person too. Maybe he's having difficulty at home and is distracted, or maybe he sees you as being ineffective right now. If it has something to do with your job performance, you'd want to know this so you could do whatever it takes to get a raise. Who knows? But what we do know are the facts: You haven't gotten a raise and you don't know why. Bringing it to your manager's attention may get you that much closer to getting a raise and that seems to be your ultimate goal right now."

Allison initially had some trouble accepting this, but she considered her friend's advice for much of the day and finally moved past the "shoulds" in her mind. The very next day, she went to her boss and asked for a raise. He thanked her for coming to him and apologized for not speaking with her earlier. He mentioned that he'd noticed her work slipping, but he was happy to know that she was interested in getting ahead. They put together a performance plan, and within three months Allison was back on track and had gotten a raise.

---

explore: What Are Your Inner Rules?

Explore what some of your inner rules might be. Generally, an inner rule or judgment is a feeling that you or someone else should do something in a certain way. It may also involve thinking that others should know about your wants or needs without you having to express them. Describe some examples from your own life where inner rules or judgments led to disappointment or increased anxiety, or perhaps even played a role in preventing you from getting what you wanted.

_____

_____

_____

_____

_____

_____

_____

When you look closely at the workings of your mind, you may discover all kinds of inner rules about how you, others, or the world should be. You may be amazed at the number of "shoulds" you possess and how frequently you see the world in this way. Mindfulness will allow you to see this dynamic more clearly. When you recognize that you're operating under the influence of an inner rule, you have the opportunity to free yourself from this way of thinking.

Before you move on, take a moment to compassionately reflect on, acknowledge, and integrate what you learned in this exploration.

Just Do It!

Inner rules need not be weighty or highly problematic; they can also extend to minor, day-to-day decisions. By challenging your inner rules in easier, safer contexts, you'll develop awareness of how these rules operate and build confidence for challenging more significant rules. Take a moment right now to make a plan for breaking out of some of your routines and experimenting with doing things differently. Here are some examples:

- Sleep on the other side of the bed.

- Have a different breakfast than you normally do, or check out a cuisine you've never tried before.

- Eat with your opposite hand.

- Style your hair differently.

- Take another point of view from the one you normally take.

- Imagine yourself on your deathbed many years from now, looking back on your life and thinking about the things you wish you had done. Then try doing one of those things.

❁ *Planning and Reviewing Your Practice* ❁

Here are the formal practices from this chapter. Go ahead and put them on your calendar over the next week. Try to practice at least five days a week. You can either alternate the practices from day to day, or you might combine them, starting with mindful yoga and continuing with the meditation for stress and anxiety. Also schedule a time about a week from now when you'll review your practice to see how it's going.

Formal Practice

- ☐ Mindful Self-Inquiry for Stress and Anxiety

- ☐ Mindful Standing Yoga

Now you have seven informal practices to integrate into your daily life.

Informal Practice

- ☐ RAIN

- ☐ Being Mindful of Habits

- ☐ Minding Your Pain

- ☐ STOP

- ☐ Bringing the Eight Attitudes of Mindfulness into Your Life

- ☐ Weaving Mindfulness Throughout Your Day

- ☐ Mindful Eating

Formal Practice Log

Each time you do a formal practice, fill out the following log. As you fill it out, and as you look back over the previous week's practice, think about how your practice has been going. Do you notice any patterns about what works best for you? What changes could you make to sustain the discipline?

Date and practice	Time	Thoughts, feelings, and sensations that arose during this practice and how you felt afterward

Reflecting on Informal Practice

Take some time every day to reflect on at least one instance of informal practice. You can use what you learn from these reflections to deepen your daily informal practice.

Practice	What was the situation?	What did you notice before?	What did you notice after?	What did you learn?

❋ chapter 8 ❋

transforming fear through loving-kindness meditation

In this chapter, we'll expand your mindfulness practice to include loving-kindness meditation. It's like an elixir for the fearful and overwhelmed heart and can greatly enhance your work with stress, anxiety, pain, or illness. By bringing loving-kindness into your life, you'll gradually experience deeper levels of love and compassion. Loving-kindness dissolves barriers of egocentricity, greed, resentment, jealousy, and hatred, creating more spaciousness and freedom in the mind and the heart. This ancient practice involves cultivating compassion and love for yourself and then expanding those feelings out to others in ever-widening circles, eventually extending to all living beings. If you're like most people in this fast-paced world, you may tend to put caring for yourself last on your to-do list, so you may find it difficult to begin by extending compassion toward yourself. Know that it is both healing and essential to do so. You cannot fully extend compassion and love to others if you're unable to extend them to yourself.

Loving-kindness can be defined as benevolent goodwill or altruistic love. It's a boundless kind of love that softens the heart and can be compared to the sun, the moon, or the stars, as it shines on all living beings without distinction, separation, or prejudice. It is important to note that loving-kindness also incorporates other important qualities, including compassion, sympathetic joy, and equanimity. The history of loving-kindness meditation goes back more than 2,500 years to the time of the Buddha. As the story goes, a group of monks journeyed to a remote forest to do some intensive meditation practice. After setting up their forest hermitages, they settled down for meditation. However, they soon began hearing disturbing sounds, smelling terrible scents, and seeing horrific ghostly images, and their belongings were mysteriously disappearing or being scattered. At first they thought someone was playing a practical joke, but they eventually realized that no one (at least no human being) was responsible. The monks fled the haunted forest and returned to the Buddha. When the Buddha asked them why they came back, they said that they were being bothered by spirits and couldn't meditate. The Buddha taught them loving-kindness meditation as an antidote to fear and told them to go back to the same forest and send loving-kindness to the spirits.

As the monks traveled back to the forest, they practiced loving-kindness meditation. Soon they were greeted by those same spirits who had been so frightening before, but now they were transformed into something beautiful because of the loving-kindness being sent to them. The spirits warmly welcomed the monks, washed their feet, and prepared food for them. The monks chose to settle in this remote forest setting, where they lived in harmony with all sentient beings, extending loving-kindness far and near. It's said that in a very short time, all of the monks and spirits attained enlightenment.

the great unnamed epidemic: lack of self-compassion

It may sound wonderful to practice loving-kindness and feel all this love for yourself and then extend it outward, but we want to acknowledge that this may not be easy. You may not want to admit just how little compassion you have, and you may find it especially difficult to extend compassion to yourself. Meditation teacher and poet Stephen Levine often says that one of the most important paths to healing is to love ourselves (Levine 1987). Unfortunately, for many of us this is very hard to do. Both of us have spent many years working with thousands of people living with stress, anxiety, pain, and illness. All too often, it seems that so much suffering comes from the simple fact that people are much too hard on themselves. This is truly an epidemic that has never been fully acknowledged or named. In all likelihood, you probably wouldn't treat a friend the way you treat yourself. For one thing, if you did, you might not have any friends. In a past mindfulness class, a woman reflected on her internal dialogue and realized that hardly a day went by that she didn't call herself an asshole. Another woman quickly added that she calls herself an idiot every day, and then a man said he called himself stupid and worthless on a regular basis. Why do we say these things to ourselves?

Though it's hard to be sure, it seems that for at least some time early in life, most of us felt whole within ourselves and connected with the world. Observe almost any child under two years old and you'll see a being who is really full of himself or herself. Very young children have a certain kind of sovereignty based on self-acceptance. When they have to poop, they poop. When they have to pee or fart, they pee or fart. When they're unhappy, they cry, and when they're happy, they smile and laugh. Babies seem to have a sense of freedom and openness when it comes to self-expression. Sadly, somewhere along the way many of us have learned to not be okay with ourselves. How does this happen? Why are we so hard on ourselves? Is this a problem of upbringing or culture? Does it affect some people and not others?

It appears to be part of the human condition that many of us are occasionally plagued with a lack of self-love and compassion. How many times have you told yourself things like "I should have done better?" At one time or another—or perhaps quite often—you've probably felt unsure of yourself and less than confident. The fact is, nearly everyone is plagued by a nasty, small-minded, fearful critic that judges them day in and day out. Loving-kindness meditation is a useful antidote and an excellent means of cultivating inner healing. With time and practice, we can all aspire to achieve greater self-acceptance, and even self-love, as so beautifully described in the poem "Love After Love," by Derek Walcott, a Nobel Prize winner in literature:

The time will come
when, with elation,
you will greet yourself arriving
at your own door, in your own mirror,
and each will smile at the other's welcome,

and say, sit here. Eat.
You will love again the stranger who was your self.
Give wine. Give bread. Give back your heart
to itself, to the stranger who has loved you

all your life, whom you ignored
for another, who knows you by heart.
Take down the love letters from the bookshelf,

the photographs, the desperate notes,
peel your own image from the mirror.
Sit. Feast on your life.

—Derek Walcott, "Love After Love" (1976, 74)

Perhaps one of the greatest gifts you can offer yourself is self-reconciliation. Isn't it time that you acknowledge your past and understand that it has led you to this present moment? Isn't it time to open your heart to resolution and compassion? It's important to comprehend that all of your past experiences, the skillful and the less so, have been part of your life and have brought you into this present moment. As you look back into your past, use the wisdom of hindsight to understand how your actions were sometimes driven by a lack of awareness and fear. This awareness will help you develop more compassion for where you were and a better understanding of how you got to be where you are now.

As your loving-kindness practice grows, you can gradually expand compassion, reconciliation, and peace beyond yourself and eventually extend it to all living beings, opening your heart to ever-greater connection. Albert Einstein, known for his brilliant scientific intellect, was also a very wise mystic, as evidenced by this excerpt from a letter published in the *New York Post* (1972, 12):

"A human being is part of the whole, called by us the Universe, a part limited in time and space. He experiences himself, his thoughts and feelings, as something separate from the rest—a kind of optical delusion of his consciousness. This delusion is a kind of prison for us, restricting us to our personal desires and to affection for a few persons nearest to us. Our task must be to free ourselves from this prison by widening our circle of compassion to embrace all living creatures and the whole of nature in its beauty."

formal practice: Loving-Kindness Meditation

Formal loving-kindness meditation is a beautiful practice that opens the heart to love, compassion, and empathy. In this practice, it's important to get in touch with the boundless love that exists in the universe and first bring it into your own heart. After directing love and compassion toward yourself, you extend it outward, first to those who are easy to love, such as benefactors, mentors, teachers, and others who have guided or inspired you. You can begin with one person and extend to others. Next you expand to near and dear ones among your family, friends, and community in the same way, and then to neutral people, acquaintances, or strangers, like the clerk at the grocery check-out stand. Then you send loving-kindness even to difficult people, including those with whom you have conflict; this will begin the important work of neutralizing the toxic effects of harboring resentments. It's nice to close this meditation by sending loving-kindness to those experiencing physical or emotional pain or hardship. Finally, you extend loving-kindness to all living beings everywhere.

You can do loving-kindness meditation either lying down or sitting up, but if you lie down and find yourself falling asleep, try a more upright posture. Bring your full, undivided attention to this practice as you listen to the CD or read the meditation below, pausing after each paragraph. Try to practice for thirty minutes (track 21). However, if you're short on time, you'll also find a fifteen-minute version on the CD (track 20). The CD also includes a forty-five-minute version that incorporates an additional meditation on impermanence and loving-kindness (track 22).

In loving-kindness meditation, it's traditional to repeat phrases that express your love, compassion, and well-wishes. On the CD and in the text below, we've supplied phrases that work well for most people, but if these words don't resonate with you, feel free to make up your own. Also feel free to vary the phrases you use from one practice to the next.

Begin your practice by congratulating yourself that you're dedicating some precious time to meditation. May you know that this is an act of love.

As you begin to stop and become present, become aware of the body and mind and whatever is being carried within—perhaps feelings or thoughts from the day's events or whatever has been going on within you recently.

Simply allow and acknowledge whatever is within and just let it be without evaluation, judgment, or any form of analysis.

Gradually, shift the focus of awareness to the breath, breathing normally and naturally. As you breathe in, be aware of breathing in, and as you breathe out, be aware of breathing out. Just being aware of breathing.

Focus your attention upon the abdomen, feeling the belly expand with each inhalation and contract with each exhalation.

Just living life one inhalation and one exhalation at a time. Breathing in, breathing out, watching each breath appear and disappear. Just breathing.

Now bring awareness into your chest and heart area, feeling any sensations within. Just allow any waves of sensation to go wherever they need to go.

Gently bring awareness into your beating heart and reflect upon how fragile and precious life is. The heart is the gateway into deeper compassion and love for yourself, and for all beings.

All of us live with certain realities that cannot be escaped. From the wondrous and miraculous moment when you were conceived, you began the irreversible process of aging and subsequent illness, death, and separation. These are powerful reflections to meditate upon, for they open the heart to what is important.

Now feel into your own precious life with compassion, mercy, and love. You may often be critical or judgmental of yourself or otherwise hard on yourself. You may find it easier to be compassionate toward others than toward yourself. Many people would hardly want to repeat out loud to others what they tell themselves, for fear of what others would then think of them.

Feel into the powerful qualities of loving-kindness itself, a boundless, altruistic love that could be compared to the sun, the moon, or the stars, shining on all living beings without distinction, separation, or prejudice.

Bring this love into your own heart, skin, flesh, organs, bones, cells, and being. May you open to deep kindness and compassion for yourself, recognizing and accepting the imperfectly perfect being that you are.

It may be a struggle to feel loving toward yourself. Work with this by acknowledging your challenges, and then continue to open to discover what it feels like to have an experience of loving-kindness toward yourself.

Take a moment right now to open to each of the following phrases for a few minutes, letting them sink into your being:

May I be safe.
May I be healthy.
May I have ease of body and mind.
May I be at peace.

Now expand the field of loving-kindness to one or many who are your benefactors, teachers, mentors, and others who have inspired you, repeating the same phrases:

May my benefactors be safe.
May my benefactors be healthy.
May my benefactors have ease of body and mind.
May my benefactors be at peace.

Now gradually expand the field of loving-kindness to one or many who are your near and dear ones among your family, friends, and community:

May my near and dear ones be safe.
May my near and dear ones be healthy.
May my near and dear ones have ease of body and mind.
May my near and dear ones be at peace.

Now further extend the field of loving-kindness to one or many who are neutral people, acquaintances, and strangers:

May my neutral ones be safe.
May my neutral ones be healthy.
May my neutral ones have ease of body and mind.
May my neutral ones be at peace.

Now consider extending loving-kindness even to one or many who are your difficult ones, or enemies. It may seem challenging or even impossible to send loving-kindness to this group of people. With the understanding that resentments have a toxic effect on your own health and well-being, begin to neutralize these resentments by sending loving-kindness and compassion to yourself. Then reflect upon forgiveness and realize that conflict and unkindness often have their roots in fear and lack of awareness. Open your heart and extend loving-kindness to the difficult ones, and then further extend the wish that they will find the gateway into their own hearts, gaining greater awareness and transforming their fear into love. Gently and slowly send loving-kindness to the difficult ones or enemies:

> May my difficult ones be safe.
> May my difficult ones be healthy.
> May my difficult ones have ease of body and mind.
> May my difficult ones be at peace.

Now take some time to remember those less fortunate, bringing into your heart anyone you know who is experiencing physical or emotional pain. Picture these people who face difficulty or challenges experiencing more healing and peace.

Further expand this circle of healing to all beings. May all living beings experiencing sickness in the body or anguish in the mind be at peace.

Now send loving-kindness to all who are victims of natural disasters or war, and to those who are hungry or without homes. May they too be at peace.

Extend loving kindness to anyone who is feeling anxiety, stress, isolation, alienation, or hope-lessness, and to those who are addicted or lost or who have given up. May they too be at peace.

Letting none be forsaken, may those who are suffering in any way be at peace.

Build this loving-kindness energy to become as boundless as the sky and begin to radiate it to all human beings and all living beings.

Send loving-kindness to all living beings, omitting none, whether great or small, weak or strong, seen or unseen, near or far, born or yet to be born.

Send this vast love to all beings of the earth, the water, and the air, spreading loving-kindness in all directions:

> May all beings be safe.
> May all beings be healthy.
> May all beings have ease of body and mind.
> May all beings be at peace.

Now extend this love outward, without boundaries or limits, into the solar system and then further, throughout the universe. May all beings be at peace.

And then once again spread this boundless loving-kindness within yourself and then to all beings throughout the universe. May all beings be at peace.

As you begin to withdraw from the loving-kindness meditation, come back to the breath, and sensing and feeling into the whole body as you breathe in and out. Feel the entire body rising upward on an inhalation and falling downward on an exhalation. Feel the body as a single, complete organism, connected and whole.

As you come to the end of this meditation, may you share any merits you've gained with all beings. May all beings be at peace.

May you again congratulate yourself for practicing this meditation and know that it is contributing to your health and well-being. May you know that this is an act of love.

Loving-Kindness Meditation Journal

As soon as you finish your first loving-kindness meditation, write about whatever comes to mind as you reflect on your experience. What thoughts, feelings, and sensations arose as you did the loving-kindness meditation? What effect did it have on you? How does it inspire you?

_____

_____

_____

_____

_____

_____

_____

Just Do It!

Take a moment and reflect on a family member, friend, work colleague, or anyone who comes to mind. What would it be like to walk in that person's shoes for a little bit? Imagine that person's history of disappointments and losses, and also his or her history of adventures and triumphs. Step into that person's life right now. You could try this with a friend, a foe, or a stranger. What feelings do you experience in your body and mind when you reflect and connect in this way? Can you sense the bond of humanity that you share?

working with resistance: what to do when you don't feel loving

It's quite common to sometimes not feel very loving while practicing loving-kindness meditation. In actuality, loving-kindness meditation may stir up difficult thoughts, emotions, and memories, and feelings of resistance or resentment might arise as a result. This is yet another way in which practicing loving-kindness is valuable: It may illuminate that such feelings are present. By becoming aware of and acknowledging these feelings, you can include them as part of your practice and observe whether you feel inclined to move toward or away from loving-kindness. All of your internal experiences are workable as part of the practice.

After acknowledging and observing these feelings, you can use self-inquiry to investigate any resistance or resentment. What's holding you back from opening your heart to compassion and love for yourself or others? This is a powerful question to sit with and inquire into. You may discover a whole plethora of unacknowledged feelings within you that you need to investigate and reintegrate.

Extending loving-kindness to difficult people can also be extremely challenging. If it seems impossible to send loving-kindness to people you've had conflicts with, perhaps it's important to reflect upon how resentment or grudges affect your own mind, heart, and body. Do you benefit in any way from holding a grudge? How does your body feel when you do this? How does it affect your thoughts and emotions? By inquiring into resentment in this way, you may discover that resentment has a venomous effect on your own health and well-being and that an angry or hateful mind is a suffering mind. With this awareness, you can begin to neutralize those feelings—first and foremost by sending loving-kindness and compassion to yourself.

It's worthwhile to reflect on forgiveness and understand that hurtful or conflictual actions often stem from fear and lack of awareness. Zen master Norman Fisher wrote an interesting translation of the Book of Psalms from a Buddhist perspective called *Opening to You: Zen-Inspired Translations of the Psalms* (2002), in which he changed such words as "wicked" and "unrighteous" to "heedless" and "unmindful." This puts such a different spin on things. Rather than judging people, events, or even yourself as evil or bad, you can think of conflicts and other difficult interactions as unskillful actions committed when someone was unaware and probably fearful. In this way, you can begin to understand the feelings and needs behind the words and actions of your difficult ones or enemies. And if you haven't already, consider that just as you have a list of those who have hurt you, you may be on other people's lists. May we all find the gateway into our hearts and learn to transform fear into love.

A story about Abraham Lincoln illuminates the power of love: During the Civil War, Lincoln had occasion at an official reception to refer to Southerners as erring human beings, rather than foes to be exterminated. An elderly lady who was a fiery patriot rebuked him for speaking kindly of his enemies when he ought to be thinking of destroying them. Lincoln replied, "Madam, do I not destroy my enemies when I make them my friends?" (King 1981, 55). An ancient proverb from the Buddhist text the Dhammapada reflects a similar sentiment: "Hatred never ceases by hatred; it only ceases by love. This is a timeless truth" (Goldstein 2003, 125).

Loving-kindness is a powerful practice that can transform hatred and open the heart to immense realms of joy and peace. Never underestimate the power of love. It can move mountains and transform enemies into friends. Perhaps there is no greater healing than to learn to love yourself and others with an open heart.

FAQ

When I practice loving-kindness meditation, I sometimes experience contrary feelings, such as anger and sadness. As a result, I feel like I'm not doing it right and feel terrible about myself. What can I do?

First of all, know that this type of experience is very normal. This practice often reveals the places where you're holding back or feeling stuck. When this happens, open your heart to self-compassion, even if you don't feel it; this is part of the work you must do to open up to genuine love for others. As you come to appreciate and accept that you are imperfectly perfect, you can extend this attitude to others. Also try to acknowledge whatever emotions or memories arise—anger, sadness, feeling unsafe, confusion, or any other difficult emotions—and let them be. In time you will gradually integrate these feelings into your heart and experience deeper feelings of freedom and peace.

explore: Is Your Body-Mind Happy?

Be mindful of how you interact with yourself. How often do you send yourself unkind messages, such as "I'm hopeless" or "I'm worthless"? Would you ever talk to other people the way you talk to yourself? Do any of these messages increase your stress, anxiety, or unhappiness? How does that feel in your mind? How does that feel in your body—perhaps tired, tense, or achy? Take a moment to explore what comes up in your mind and body.

_____

_____

_____

_____

_____

_____

_____

In his book *Anger: Wisdom for Cooling the Flames* (2001), Thich Nhat Hahn talks about watering the seeds of our own suffering. If you tend to send yourself unkind messages (as we all seemingly do), you've probably been watering the seeds of your own suffering. What might be different in your life if you stopped doing this?

_____

_____

_____

_____

_____

_____

_____

_____

In day-to-day life, feelings of resentment may arise when you encounter difficult people and uncomfortable situations. What would it feel like to bring an open heart and beginner's mind to situations where someone is pressing your buttons? Consider a person with whom you currently have a conflict or difficult communication. Might that person's words and actions be connected to challenges he or she is facing? Take a moment to explore the positive qualities of a particular difficult person and the potential reasons for this person's seemingly unkind behavior.

_____

_____

_____

_____

_____

_____

_____

_____

Admittedly, this type of exploration isn't easy work. In fact, it can be quite difficult and humbling to purify your own mind and heart, but realize that living with suffering, pain, and lack of awareness is a much more difficult road. As you bring the light of awareness to your own dark side, realize that everyone has an internal shadow or bogeymen, and that this is actually the fertilizer that feeds our growth. Exploring the messages you tell yourself is a powerful first step to greater freedom. With awareness, compassion grows. May the light of awareness and compassion set you free.

Before you move on, take a moment to compassionately reflect on, acknowledge, and integrate what you just wrote.

---

informal practice: Loving-Kindness in Daily Life

You can informally extend loving-kindness to various people in the moment throughout your day. You may be sitting with your partner and choose to extend loving-kindness wishes to him or her. Or maybe you're having difficulty with someone at some point in your day; instead of reacting with fear, anger, aggression, or isolation, choose to extend loving-kindness to that person. Or say you're waiting in line at the supermarket or post office; you could choose to extend loving-kindness to someone who works there. If you're at a ball game or other public event, you could even send loving-kindness out to everyone in the crowd. The point is that you can practice loving-kindness informally—anytime, anywhere. So sprinkle a few informal loving-kindness practices throughout your day. Notice what it feels like to open your heart to others and how this changes the way you think and feel about others, yourself, and things in general.

 Planning and Reviewing Your Practice

Schedule the formal practices below for the next week, being sure to include walking meditation or mindful yoga. Try to practice at least five days a week. You can either alternate the practices from day to day, or you might combine them, starting with mindful yoga or walking meditation and continuing with loving-kindness meditation. Also schedule a time about a week from now when you'll review your practice to see how it's going.

Formal Practices

☐ Loving-Kindness Meditation

☐ Walking Meditation

☐ Mindful Yoga

Now you have eight informal practices to integrate into your daily life.

Informal Practices

☐   Loving-Kindness in Daily Life

☐   RAIN

☐   Being Mindful of Habits

☐   Minding Your Pain

☐   STOP

☐   Bringing the Eight Attitudes of Mindfulness into Your Life

☐   Weaving Mindfulness Throughout Your Day

☐   Mindful Eating

Formal Practice Log

Each time you do a formal practice, fill out the following log. As you fill it out, and as you look back over the previous week's practice, think about how your practice has been going. Do you notice any patterns about what works best for you? What changes could you make to sustain the discipline?

Date and practice	Time	Thoughts, feelings, and sensations that arose during this practice and how you felt afterward

Reflecting on Informal Practice

Take some time every day to reflect on at least one instance of informal practice. You can use what you learn from these reflections to deepen your daily informal practice.

Practice	What was the situation?	What did you notice before?	What did you notice after?	What did you learn?

interpersonal mindfulness

Up to this point, you've learned more about *intrapersonal* mindfulness—being nonjudgmentally present to the orchestra of thoughts, feelings, and sensations occurring within you. This chapter turns the focus to *interpersonal* mindfulness—bringing nonjudgmental present moment awareness to your interactions with others. You'll learn a bit about how the person you are today may be influenced by early childhood experiences, such as your connection or disconnection with your parents or caregivers. Then we'll introduce you to the qualities of interpersonal mindfulness, the art of mindful communication and listening, and how to apply interpersonal mindfulness at home and at work to improve your relationships between yourself and others.

Human beings are social animals, and most of us spend a great deal of time interacting with others, in all of their individual complexity and uniqueness. Each person you interact with—children, parents, siblings, bosses, friends, colleagues, neighbors, and even your "difficult ones," the people with whom you have conflict or other challenges—provides a doorway into a new world. To the extent that you feel separate from others, realize that we all share the common experience of being human. Each of us is born into this world and accumulates stories of courage and fear, joy and sorrow, pleasure and pain, gifts and losses. However, despite these commonalities, people can also be an enormous source of stress in life. They can be demanding, pushy, threatening, irresponsible, uncooperative, and insensitive. Sometimes, those you're most intimate with or closest to can be the greatest source of stress, perhaps because you feel more responsible for their well-being, or maybe they know just the right buttons to push.

where relationship patterns begin

Just as you've developed deeply ingrained habitual styles of thinking that can keep you stuck in a stress reaction, such as catastrophizing, exaggerating negative thoughts or feelings, and blaming, you've also developed habitual ways of interacting with others. Many of these behaviors developed in response to some of your earliest exposure to relationships—interactions with your parents or caregivers. Unfortunately, if those patterns of behavior are based on dysfunctional parent-child relationships, this may result in dysfunctional relationships with family, friends, or coworkers in your life now.

For example, if your parents didn't give you a good model for how to handle conflict, you may not handle conflict resolution very well today. When conflict arises, you may feel you'd do almost anything to try to avoid the uncomfortable emotions that are inherent in conflict. Perhaps you developed a passive style around conflict, or maybe you put others' needs before your own or feel incapable of saying no, leaving you overwhelmed, overcommitted, and stressed-out. On the flip side, you may feel at home with conflict and constantly create it, either because that's the way you learned how to make emotional contact with others or because it gives you a sense of power. The problem is, aggressive behavior leaves many hurt feelings in its wake, especially if you take advantage of others or bully or demean them. It's all too easy to get swept up in cycles of reactivity to the point where the relationship gets stuck in a downward spiral.

Conflicts in current relationships can lead to uncomfortable emotions, and there's a good chance that the situation could trigger memories or feelings associated with past wounds stemming from old, dysfunctional ways of relating. When you feel trapped or threatened, you're likely to fall into old patterns of reactivity that you've rehearsed time and time again since childhood. As we seek out love, it's helpful to understand the internal barriers that may stand in the way—barriers that often begin to form under the influence of our earliest relationships. As children, we depend on our parents or caregivers for security and stability, but they aren't always able to tune in to our needs.

Where relationship patterns began isn't pop psychology; it's based on theory and research. Psychiatrist and psychoanalyst John Bowlby (1969) first used the word "attachment" when he theorized that children are more likely to feel secure, connected, and loved if their parents are able to be attuned, in the present moment, to the child's internal world of emotions and needs. In the decades that followed, psychologists studied infants and discovered that attachment style may vary from infant to infant, and that while some attachment styles may be coupled with a sense of security and safety, other attachment styles may be paradoxically coupled with insecurity and anxiety (Ainsworth et al. 1978; Main and Solomon 1986). Neuroscientists are finding that attachment styles also affect the brain. In *Affect Dysregulation and Disorders of the Self* (2003), psychologist and neuroscientist Allan Schore, Ph.D., focuses on how attachment produces structural changes in the brain during the first two years of life. He says that insensitive parenting can affect children's ability to regulate their emotions and that they may carry this dysfunction with them throughout their lives. In *The Mindful Brain* (2007), Daniel Siegel, MD, writes that when parent and child are attuned, the outcome is a state of resonance that allows the child to "feel felt." This state of resonance helps build regulatory circuits in the brain that support the child's resilience and ability to engage and connect in meaningful, empathic relationships later in life.

What does this have to do with you as an adult? More recent research has found that the attachment status current parents had to their own parents predicts, with high accuracy, the attachment their children will have with them (van Ijzendoorn 1995). As adults, those who experienced insecure attachment as children generally have more difficulty managing their emotions and dealing with the curveballs that life throws (Shaver and Mikulincer 2002). However, it's important to note that having insecure attachment as a child doesn't doom your adult relationships. Even if you experienced insecure attachment as a child, you can shift this pattern in adulthood (Main and Goldwyn 1998).

While most parents do the best they can with the resources they have, internal and otherwise, too often there's a lack of attunement and resonance, which leaves the child feeling insecure in the relationship. For example, if your parents were emotionally unavailable as a result of being preoccupied with their own lives or struggles in their relationship, you may have adapted by dismissing the importance of emotions and relationships, trying not to be dependent on them, and developing an internal narrative that you don't need to rely on other people. Or if attunement and resonance weren't consistently present during your childhood, you may have ended up feeling confused and suspicious about relationships. As an adult, you may be riddled with worries about whether your partner will reciprocate your feelings, or you may be reluctant to engage intimately. If either of your parents acted out with frightening or abusive behavior, you may have lived in a state of fear, often feeling compelled to flee, yet also wanting your parent to soothe you. In this case, you may not only feel a sense of confusion around emotions and relationships, you may even act as a caregiver when things get difficult, trying to forestall difficult interactions by taking care of the other person's needs at your own expense.

The good news is, whatever your upbringing and early influences, mindfulness gives you the ability to recognize and understand your past by acknowledging and validating your experiences. This *intrapersonal attunement*—attunement and resonance with yourself—allows you to feel secure and open to your thoughts, feelings, and emotions (Siegel 2007, 2009). This internal awareness and resonance will strengthen you and help you feel secure enough to be present to others' feelings with patience, empathy, and wisdom, whether you're relating to family, friends, coworkers, strangers, or even difficult people. In this way, intrapersonal attunement opens the door to interpersonal attunement and resonance, which will improve all of your relationships.

❋ Elisha's Story: Hiding Under the Table

When I was six years old my parents got divorced. When they first came and told us three kids about it, I just stood there without a tear in my eye but with anger in my heart. My mom asked, "What's going on, Elisha? Do you understand what's happening?" I angrily retorted, "Yeah, what do you want me to do, bang my head against the wall so I'll cry?" Of course I was hurt and angry; my foundation—what I had known to be my family—was being ripped away from under me.

I started acting out. One way I did was at restaurants. It made me angry that we would spend money we didn't have to go to a restaurant when I thought we could just as easily cook at home. When we left the house to go out to eat, my family would have to drag me to the car as I pouted, and I spent much of the time at restaurants under the table in protest of spending the money.

Years later, I found that when my wife and I got into an argument, instead of bringing awareness to the situation and connecting with her around it, I sometimes reacted by numbing out emotionally, cleaning the house, turning on the TV, and otherwise distracting myself. I felt helpless and just didn't want to deal with it. One day when I went to therapy and described what had happened, my therapist said, "When you get angry, you still hide under the table." That's how I coped as a child, and at times that's how I was coping when I got upset with my wife. When I finally realized how my experiences as a child were influencing my marriage, I was more present to this cycle of reaction and began to shift from avoiding my pain to approaching it. This not only helped me feel more secure, it also allowed me to feel even more connected with my wife. At times I still catch myself hiding under the table, but I'm usually able to see it sooner. Then I can smile and embrace the little boy inside me, and let him know that things will be all right.

qualities of interpersonal mindfulness

Even in the most difficult interactions, where you may feel threatened, angry, and fearful, you can significantly improve the relationship by bringing interpersonal mindfulness to the situation. As we mentioned earlier, the practice of mindfulness is like cultivating a garden; certain qualities and conditions must be present in order for mindfulness to grow. In chapter 3 we presented eight attitudes essential to the practice of mindfulness. Similarly, it's important to attend to relationships if they are to flourish and be vibrant. And when relationships are strained or difficult, bringing interpersonal mindfulness to the situation can potentially prevent them from withering away or blowing up.

Here are six qualities that we consider essential in cultivating interpersonal mindfulness and dramatically improving your relationships:

- **Openness.** Similar to beginner's mind, this is a quality where you're open to seeing the other person and the relationship as new and fresh, and where you're open to the other person's perspective. Being closed-off or defensive is definitely a barrier to an open heart and mind! To cultivate openness, notice your first thought or judgment about what others are saying or doing, then imagine it as just one perspective—one slice on a pie chart, not the entire circle. Imagine filling in that pie with other perspectives, each holding equal value.

- **Empathy.** This is a quality of actually identifying with another's feelings—emotionally putting yourself in someone else's shoes. The first step is to acknowledge and experience your own feelings; only then can you do this with another person. To cultivate this quality, practice mindfulness of your own emotions, getting in touch with them and then tapping into specific emotions when you sense that others are feeling them. You may be inclined to trust your intuition in respect to how others are feeling, and this can be effective. However, if you're at all uncertain, it's generally a good practice to simply ask. If you struggle with empathy, perhaps it will help to realize that in our hearts, we all want certain basic things: to be accepted, to be loved, and to feel secure.

- **Compassion.** This is a quality that combines empathy with an understanding of the position the other person is in and a desire to ease the person's suffering. To cultivate this quality, allow yourself to imagine the sorrows and pains that the person holds. During this life, they've certainly experienced disappointments, failures, and losses, and some of these wounds may be so deep that the person may not feel safe sharing about them. Imagine the person as your own child, feeling frightened and in pain, and consider how you'd comfort him or her.

- **Loving-kindness.** This is a quality where you truly wish another well—to be healthy, safe from harm, and free from fear. As you worked with loving-kindness in chapter 8, you may have experienced that this is easier said than done with your "difficult ones." To cultivate loving-kindness, again imagine the other person as your own child and consider how you would extend these well-wishes for him or her. Imagine how you'd want to see the person bring his or her being into this world.

- **Sympathetic joy.** This is a quality where you delight in the happiness and joy of others. It's the opposite of jealousy, envy, and resentment. To cultivate this quality, imagine the other person growing up and reflect on the joy and adventure the person has experienced, along with the courage and strength he or she has brought to overcoming challenges in life. Sympathetic joy is possible regardless of the person's circumstances; simply realize that inner resources of joy are available to everyone and extend your wish that the other person might access this joy.

- **Equanimity.** This is a quality of wisdom, an evenness and steadiness of mind that comprehends the nature of change. Equanimity gives you more balance and composure in understanding the interconnectedness of all life. Like most people, you may treat others differently based on your perceptions of them. You might treat a coworker with care and be unpleasant with a post office clerk because you were in a rush. Realize that all relationships have inherent value, and that all human beings deserve to be treated with the consideration inherent in the five previous qualities. To cultivate this quality, imagine the other person's face as that of a parent, a friend, a lover, a child, or a student. This will help you see the person as someone who, like all of us, simply wants and needs kindness and love.

---

explore: Creating Connection

Creating connection with others is a process. Imagine a person you care about sitting right in front of you. Go ahead and reread the description of each quality above, and after reading each quality, close your eyes and imagine looking at and interacting with this person with a focus on that quality. When you're finished with each one, write down what came up for you.

Openness

_____

_____

_____

_____

_____

Empathy

_____

_____

_____

_____

_____

Compassion

_____

_____

_____

_____

_____

Loving-Kindness

_____

_____

_____

_____

_____

Sympathetic Joy

_____

_____

_____

_____

Equanimity

_____

_____

_____

_____

Holding these six interpersonal qualities in mind—reflecting on them and cultivating them according to your best understanding—will nourish, support, and strengthen your connections with other people. Developing these qualities is a way to channel your energies in building stronger and healthier relationships. These attitudes are interdependent; each influences the others, and by cultivating one you enhance all of them.

Before you move on, take a few moments to connect with your breath and mindfully reflect on what you just wrote, compassionately acknowledging, validating, and integrating everything you learned from this exploration.

mindful communication

Communication is the process of connecting with others or ourselves with our minds and bodies, either verbally, nonverbally, or both. You've probably had communications with others that have left you feeling connected, respected, and loved, while other interactions have left you feeling disconnected, disregarded, or frustrated. When you feel threatened, stress and fear often arise, and in an effort to avoid this discomfort you may react in ways that don't serve the relationship, you, or the other person. You may stop listening, have difficulty clearly expressing your emotions and needs, or fall into reactive mind traps of blaming, criticizing, or judging, which usually makes others feel defensive and escalates the situation. As this cycle continues, you can become increasingly fearful, angry, self-absorbed, and fixated on your own views and feelings. Resistance and defensiveness increase, empathy flies out the window, and attunement and resonance, which are so important for healthy communication, seem like a distant dream.

Fortunately, you can turn this cycle around by cultivating skills for more effective communication, increasing the likelihood of meaningful and satisfying interactions. As you bring mindfulness to communication, paying attention to your thoughts, feelings, and sensations, you'll create the space to intentionally respond to others' actions rather than reacting to them in habitual ways. One of the most fundamental of these skills is the art of mindful listening.

The Art of Mindful Listening

You may have heard the saying "We were given two ears and one mouth so we can listen twice as much as we talk." As a kid you may have rolled your eyes when your parents once again said, "Are you listening to me?" As kids, many of us didn't listen, and we may have resented the question. In adult relationships, this can translate into continued lack of attention, coupled with a halfhearted rehashing of the few words that seeped into your ears. In fact, both people may be relating in this way, leading to interactions characterized by feelings of disconnection, frustration, and pain. As an old Spanish proverb says, "Two great talkers will not travel far together." We all want to be heard. It's essential to feeling understood, accepted, and loved. When we sense that others are truly listening, our fears and defenses tend to fade away, paving the way for greater connection, empathy, and peace in the relationship.

Hearing vs. Listening

Unfortunately, while most of us feel like we're *hearing* others, we often aren't actually *listening*. Let's really examine the distinction between hearing and listening. Hearing is a passive physiological process in which your ears take in the vibration of sounds without deliberate and thoughtful attention. Listening, on the other hand, is an active mental process where you intentionally and thoughtfully pay attention to the message the other person is conveying. As such, it involves also attending to cues other than the auditory stimuli of the words being spoken—cues like body language, tone, or facial expression. This means hearing isn't a choice, but listening is.

Because genuine communication is so rewarding, it's worth considering why we spend so much time hearing without listening. There are a number of potential reasons. If you're like most people, you simply have too much to listen to in your environment. Indeed, it seems that from the day we're born, we begin to make micro decisions about who and what to pay attention to, and many of these decisions occur without conscious thought or deliberation. Over time, we settle into a groove and often choose to listen to the messages that reinforce how we feel about things. Take politics, for example. Whether conservative or liberal, most people listen to messages and media that reinforce their opinions and express utter disdain for those that represent "the other side." And when they do hear messages presented by the other side, they may not really listen to them. In truth, relationships have a lot in common with politics; they may be a process of negotiating between conflicting needs, desires, and opinions. And while there are often messages coming from both sides, each may not truly take in the other's message.

Emotions and Listening

Emotions also have an enormous influence on what we listen to and how we listen. If you're feeling happy, you'll tend to filter out unpleasant messages and listen to those you interpret as pleasant. On the other hand, if you're feeling depressed or anxious, you'll tend to listen to the unpleasant messages while ignoring the pleasant ones. When you're confronted with a situation that you interpret as threatening, you're likely to get stressed and feel fear or anger. When the fight, flight, or freeze response kicks in, your mind may jump into overdrive. Instead of listening, you may be trying to figure out how to fix the situation or run away from it, or you may feel paralyzed or frozen.

Being mindful allows you to notice your reactions and shift back to the present, acknowledging your feelings and entering the mode of being, rather than doing. As you nonjudgmentally approach your discomfort and let it be, you can harness the qualities of interpersonal mindfulness, shifting to a place of empathy, compassion, and connection to the other person. By bringing intention to listening to others, including any pain and suffering they're experiencing, you can see how their history of losses and wounds may play a role in how they react. This allows you to respond with empathy, acknowledging the pain that others express. By listening mindfully, you're also more likely to see any gaps in your understanding so that you can ask questions to clarify any confusion.

This type of mindful interaction allows the other person to "feel felt," creating more attunement and resonance and dissipating any fear or anger that may have been influencing the interaction. Remember, those who are aggressive often act that way due to feeling insecure, threatened, or fearful. When people feel listened to, they feel more connected and less on guard or defensive.

In our workshops we often divide participants into groups of three or four to practice mindful listening. The primary instruction is that when one person is talking, the others listen without inter-rupting. One participant, George, lived a particularly hectic life, juggling ten-hour workdays, marriage, and three kids. He often relied on multitasking to help him manage everything. For example, when he was at the dinner table or helping one of his kids with homework, he might respond to texts from the office to help lighten his load the next day. This "solution" was having a negative impact on the quality of time he spent with his family and often created more stress and difficulty.

After practicing mindful listening in class, George went home and decided to practice it with his son Andrew. He turned off his cell phone and simply listened as Andrew told him about a boy who was bullying him and how afraid he was. As George took this in without interrupting, he recalled how he too was bullied when he was young and how that felt. In that moment, he noticed feelings of love and empathy for his little boy, and a connection to him that he hadn't been aware of for quite some time. When Andrew finished talking, George shared his own story and told Andrew that he loved him. He realized later that this was the first time he had ever expressed his love verbally. Andrew tearfully told George he loved him too, and as George held him close, he felt his own tears begin to well up—tears of love and compassion, and of appreciation for this mindful and precious moment.

Mindful listening is truly an art, and cultivating it takes practice. With time, you'll abandon your habitual filters and take in deeper messages that you never knew were there. One of them may be how truly loved you are.

informal practice: Mindful Listening

When someone is speaking to you, see if you can pay attention and not interrupt until the other person is completely finished speaking.

Notice when your mind begins to wander off, thinking about what you need to do later that day, some grievance from the past, the brilliant counterargument that you want to make, or wherever else it may go. When this happens, just become aware of it, then intentionally bring your attention back to listening. Remember, when people feel listened to, not only do they feel more connected to you, they also feel less on guard or defensive. This creates the space for a much more fruitful dialogue and connection. It also opens you up to take in so much more of what the other person is saying, since the invaluable resource of your attention is no longer as devoted to what's going on in your head. In doing this practice, you may find that you take in much more of life than you used to. See if you can practice this with an attitude of curiosity.

When the person has finished speaking, take a breath before you respond.

Remember, you won't be perfect at this, so every time you aren't able to listen mindfully, forgive yourself and use that moment as an insight to strengthen your practice of listening mindfully. You may do this again and again.

the aikido of communication

Mindfulness-based stress reduction programs draw on awareness exercises adapted from aikido, a Japanese martial art created by Morihei Ueshiba. Aikido, which has been called an art of peacemaking, is based on courage, wisdom, love, and connection. In MBSR, an aspect of aikido is taught to help people break out of habitual reactions to threatening, emotional, or stressful interaction and instead blend with the other's energy in a way that reduces the conflict and does no harm to you or the other.

It's often in our most intimate relationships that we are harshest with one another. All too often, people lash out at those closest to them until one day the person bearing the brunt of this wakes up and says, "I can't take this anymore. I want out." Whether you're relating to your intimate partner, a family member, a friend, your boss, or a stranger, there are endless opportunities to be on the receiving end of a communication that's hurtful or difficult to accept. If you're operating on autopilot, you can easily spin into a fight, flight, or freeze reaction. If the cycle isn't broken, your thoughts, emotions, and sensations build on one another until you find yourself avoiding, becoming passive-aggressive, identifying yourself as a victim, or even becoming downright aggressive and confrontational. This effectively closes the door to understanding and reconciliation.

Ignoring or avoiding the attack is a passive strategy that may provide temporary relief, but it's likely to increase the other person's frustration and therefore come back to bite you later. Dealing with others in a passive-aggressive way is often very confusing to them and generally escalates the conflict. It's also important to note that by submitting to a verbal attack and just allowing others to get their way without standing up for yourself, you're being passive or a victim, and over time it chips away at your self-respect and leaves you feeling like a doormat. This is one reason the purely aggressive strategy of fighting back is so common. It feels good to stand up for yourself because it gives you a sense of self-respect. Plus, you're definitely connecting with the other person, even if it isn't in a way that promotes attunement and understanding, and we thrive on connection with others.

In aikido, a specific physical movement called entering and blending allows you to respond to an attack with a skillful deflection so that neither you nor the aggressor is hurt. This movement first neutralizes the aggressive action and then begins to transform it. In the realm of communication, this approach offers an alternative to avoidance, passive-aggression, victim behavior, and pure aggression. Entering and blending in communication is a more skillful way of interacting that leads to attunement and connection. While it's akin to being assertive, it goes beyond that to create harmony in the relationship. Let's take a look at the specifics of how you accomplish this:

- **Align.** In aikido, you start by approaching and entering the interaction instead of avoiding or submitting to the other person's attack. One way to do this is by understanding that the aggressor is feeling imbalanced and ill at ease. Try putting yourself in the other person's shoes, asking yourself how you would feel if you were in the person's situation at that very moment. Consider what struggles may have brought the person to this difficult situation. When aligning, it's critical to practice mindful listening—not just to the words, but also to the emotions behind them, which are often reflected in tone of voice. If you're unclear about the reason for the attack, sincerely ask about the other person's feelings and beliefs about the situation. You might say, "I want to understand your point of view better. Tell me more about what's going on." This will provide more clarity so that you can better align yourself. It also sows the seeds of empathy, compassion, and attunement.

- **Agree.** Finding areas you can agree on supports the alignment, as both people begin to look in the same direction. Mindful listening will help you identify if you have any worries, emotions, or needs that resonate with what the other person is feeling. Don't make things up that aren't true just to put on an appearance of empathizing; see if you can genuinely validate the person's feelings in light of the situation. You might say something like, "I'm also concerned about our finances. Being short on money makes me scared and nervous too" or "If I were treated that way, I'd be angry too" or "I'm also disappointed about this situation." Notice how each of these examples uses statements starting with "I." Remember to speak only for yourself. People tend to get defensive when they think you're blaming them.

- **Redirect.** This is where you begin to move the interaction in a more positive direction. You might say, "We're both disappointed about the situation. What can we do to make it better?" Instead of being on opposing sides, now the two of you are teaming up and working together to find a way to resolve the situation.

- **Resolve.** This doesn't necessarily imply a resolution. In this stage you don't know where the situation is going to go, but at least you're connected and looking in the same direction. Now you can begin exploring what a mutually agreeable compromise might be, or you might just agree to disagree. You might say, "If I ate out less, could we get a housekeeper so we could spend more time together?" You can offer a compromise for a short period of time and commit to revisiting it to see if it's working out for both parties. If you're unable to agree on anything, you may want to go back to exploring what the problem is and find things to agree on again.

When you make the decision to align with the other person's energy, you must be centered and mindful of your own state, even if anger or fear is there. One way to notice if you're reacting is by paying attention to your body. If anything is stiff or tense, you're probably reacting to your own discomfort and trying to avoid or ignore it. Use these physical sensations as a cue to acknowledge whatever thoughts and feelings are there, and bring yourself to the present by tuning in to the breath as it rises and falls. As you become centered and present, you make space to respond mindfully and with greater flexibility and creativity, rather than mindlessly reacting. As always, be patient and compassionate with yourself. It will take time and practice to develop your skill in the aikido of communication. In the beginning, you may find that you continue to react with fear or anger. When this happens, let it be and simply invite yourself to engage in the process of entering and blending.

It's also important to acknowledge that sometimes people will dig their heels in so deep that there can't be a resolution to the problem at that time. You may not even be able to agree on what the problem is, and your beliefs may seem fundamentally different. In the end, you may have to agree to disagree. If emotions are too high, it's probably best if both of you take some time and space to take care of your fear or anger, and then come back to the table when you both feel calmer. Sometimes just knowing when to back away and when to move toward the other person is the wisdom needed for a healthy relationship. Walking away can be a reflection of having the insight to recognize that at the moment resolution may not be possible.

By helping you learn how to align, agree, redirect, and eventually resolve, the aikido of communication moves beyond assertiveness and even beyond standing up for yourself with self-respect. It allows you to diffuse emotionally charged situations while emphasizing connection, empathy, compassion, and harmony.

explore: Identifying Habitual Patterns in Your Current Relationships

Do any of the styles of communication discussed above—avoidance, passive-aggressiveness, victim behavior, downright aggression, assertiveness, or blending—seem familiar to you? Do you have any habitual ways of reacting with certain people? Use the space below to write about any such relationships that come to mind. For example, if you notice yourself falling into victim behavior frequently with a specific person, write about how those interactions happen. Who says what, and what thoughts, feelings, and sensations arise? What's the end result? Or if you find yourself being aggressive or assertive with a certain person, write about that. Getting a bird's-eye view of your communication styles helps you increase awareness so that you can begin to step out of these habitual patterns.

_____

_____

_____

_____

_____

_____

_____

_____

May you cultivate the awareness to recognize habitual patterns that support unhealthy relationships and thereby create the space to make a change.

Before you move on, take a moment to connect with your breath and mindfully reflect on what you just wrote, compassionately acknowledging, validating, and integrating what you learned.

FAQ

How can I work with my fears about interpersonal communication?

Many of us have fears of not being accepted by others. This may happen when our feelings have been hurt or when we feel unseen and unacknowledged. It takes courage to open your heart when you feel scared and unsure of yourself. An important part of the solution is to spend time honoring, working with, and healing wounds from the past. Practicing mindfulness, self-compassion, and loving-kindness will be very helpful. Perhaps the greatest key to friendship and connection lies in the ability to deeply listen with interest, care, and emotional resonance. Many of us have a deep yearning to be heard, and often one of the greatest gifts we can offer to others is to listen.

mindfulness in important relationships

In a world where it's so easy to feel disconnected and defended, poet, author, and teacher Stephen Levine asks some searching questions: "If you were going to die soon and had only one phone call you could make, who would you call and what would you say? And why are you waiting?" (Jarski 2007, 123). Why do we wait to share our feelings with those we care about? It certainly doesn't help that, over time, we tend to become so absorbed with our own problems and worries that this illusion of separateness continues to grow. In 1951, David Bohm wrote *Quantum Theory*, a book that redefined not only the way we understand physics, but also the way we see relationships. He said that if you were able to separate an atomic particle into two subunits and send them to opposite ends of the world, or even the universe, changing the spin of one would instantly change the spin of the other. Since that time, this theory, known as nonlocality, has been repeatedly validated in empirical studies, leading us closer to the understanding that we are all literally interconnected. How might putting a mindful spin on your actions affect your everyday relationships?

In our closest relationships, it can be tempting to create a sort of balance sheet where we keep score of who has spent time loving and who hasn't. You might ask yourself whether loved ones have given you as much as you've given them. It may seem like a fair enough question, but it begins to sow the seeds of resentment and separateness. If you look at relationships this way, you might even start testing people in passive-aggressive ways to see if they really do love you. Sometimes this leads to the dark side of creating your own reality: As you look for problems, you start to distance yourself emotionally, driving a wedge into the relationship. As you become absorbed in your own worries and resentments, you may react accordingly, even if the other person doesn't feel or think as you imagine they do.

Mindfulness is the key to turning this situation around. In an interesting approach pioneered by psychologist James Carson and colleagues (2006), partners in romantic relationships participate in a modified mindfulness-based stress reduction program aimed at developing interpersonal mindfulness skills. Evaluation of the program indicates that these couples have greater acceptance and happiness within the relationship and are better able to handle the stressful situations that inevitably arise in any close relationship. One obvious reason for this is that mindfulness fosters empathy, which leads to greater understanding and connection. When people feel understood and connected, the winds of reactivity die down. When you're mindful in the relationship, you're more likely to notice any fear that arises. With this awareness, you can choose to open your heart instead of reacting by avoiding, submitting, or fighting back.

If it feels scary to open your heart, know that you aren't alone. Many people feel this way, for a variety of reasons. Maybe when you were a child your parents weren't attuned to you; that was painful, and you may fear that all close relationships will follow this pattern. Or maybe your heart has been broken so many times that you fear being rejected or abandoned once again. Rather than risk becoming vulnerable, you avoid expressing love to partners or friends. Fear can block you from having the relationships you truly want to have.

explore: Why Might You Be Afraid to Love or Be Loved?

So many factors go into our automatic defenses against loving others or accepting their love. Perhaps your parents didn't acknowledge your feelings as a child, so you adapted by not considering them important. Maybe you've been hurt many times before and fear being hurt again. Think of some of your closer

interpersonal mindfulness

relationships and really explore what may be getting in the way of being more open or expressing how you feel.

_____

_____

_____

_____

_____

_____

_____

In doing this exploration, you may come to realize that the walls of fear block the path to your heart. May you cultivate a sense of compassion for yourself and know that through practicing mindfulness, you can create the space for the fear to come and go and experience the freedom to let love in if you choose to do so.

Before you move on, take a few moments to connect with your breath and mindfully reflect on what you just wrote, compassionately acknowledging, validating, and integrating everything you learned from this exploration.

mindfulness in work relationships

Everything you've read and worked with in this chapter can be brought into the workplace. The truth is, many of us spend the majority of our waking hours at work, and this is where many of our daily interactions take place. It's no secret that work can be highly stressful, which can make you feel less tolerant of dealing with difficult people. Two-thirds of both men and women say that work has a significant effect on their stress levels (American Psychological Association 2004), and stress-related claims add up to over $300 billion dollars annually—just for corporations (American Institute of Stress 2009). It seems that many people are being asked to do more work in less time, leaving them feeling exhausted, unfocused, unproductive, unhealthy, and burnt-out.

When we get caught up in busy routines at work, it's all too easy to go on autopilot without even realizing it. Sometimes the focus on productivity and deadlines can cause us to forget that those we work with are human and want to be listened to and respected. Joe, a thirty-two-year-old software engineer, is a case in point. He dreaded going to work because of the tension he felt with his boss, who had gotten into a pattern of nagging him for end-of-day reports. He complied begrudgingly, and every time he was called into her office, he immediately felt tense and irritated. Although he pretended to listen to her, he often whistled a tune in his head as she spoke to him.

Eventually, this stress caused him to sign up for a mindfulness program. As he began to work with mindfulness in his own life, he saw how he could bring this approach into the workplace, and into his interactions and relationship with his boss. Even just this realization helped him become open to more possibilities as to why she might be irritable. As he considered that she probably had her own disappointments, losses, and wounds in life, she became more human to him. He started really listening to her and discovered that much of what she said and how she said it conveyed the stress of her job, and that what he had seen as nagging was less about him and more about fears in regard to her own performance. Then he did something completely different: He told his boss that he admired her for being able to handle such big responsibilities. She thanked him and then shared that she had been feeling overwhelmed in recent months because her mother had been in and out of the hospital for an aggressive cancer. Joe noticed that he felt empathy for her, and even loving-kindness, so he silently wished her health, happiness, and safety. From that day on, when he walked down the hall to her office he noticed that he wasn't tense and that his breathing was steady. He also noticed that he actually smiled at her at times, and that she seemed more pleasant in their interactions.

Just Do It—or *Not*!

Just Do It: As much as we'd like to believe people are mind readers, this just isn't the case. Pick one of the people you made notes about as you explored why you might be afraid to love or be loved, then either get in touch with that person now or set a date to constructively and compassionately let him or her know your feelings either in person, by phone, or by e-mail. If you notice fear, just acknowledge its presence, let it be, and gently bring your attention back to making this happen. This can be a difficult task, so be kind to yourself during the process. You can do it!

Just Don't Do It: Sometimes we need to discern whether or not it's skillful to seek resolution with another person. Sometimes it isn't the right time to talk, or it may never be the right time to talk. If this is the case, making peace within is what matters most. Understand that resolution can occur even if you don't talk with the other person; it can take place within your own heart. Take a moment and reflect on whether the contact will be beneficial to you or not.

mindfulness with difficult people

No matter how hard you try, some people are just difficult. However, before you wash your hands of them, bear in mind that some of the greatest spiritual teachers would tell you that difficult people are the best teachers of all. If that seems counterintuitive, consider this: You'll never be fully free, loving, and flexible if you don't become intimate with the discomfort you're reacting to. Difficult people provide you with an excellent opportunity to notice your aversions and develop more expansive and flexible interpersonal mindfulness. Consider how you might use a difficult interaction as an opportunity to be aware of discomfort without reacting by avoiding, becoming passive-aggressive, feeling like a victim, or being downright aggressive. You can hone your skills in the aikido of communication with this person. Indeed, difficult people will help you expand your skills by pushing you to the edge of your comfort zone—a place you might not otherwise choose to visit. Remember, despite our differences, there's a commonality to the human experience. We all want to love and be loved. Take a step back from your preconceived notions and habitual reactions so that you can see this person as a fellow human being with wounds, losses, and disappointments. View your interactions with difficult people not as an affliction, but as an opportunity to cultivate loving-kindness and practice interpersonal mindfulness. It may not be easy, but it will probably be extremely worthwhile.

❧ *Planning and Reviewing Your Practice* ❧

At this point, you can schedule any of the meditation practices you've learned in this workbook for at least five days this week. Also schedule a time about a week from now when you'll review your practice to see how it's going.

Formal Practices

☐   Mindful Breathing

☐   Walking Meditation

☐   Body Scan

☐   Sitting Meditation

☐   Mindful Yoga

☐   Mindful Self-Inquiry for Stress and Anxiety

☐   Loving-Kindness Meditation

Now you have nine informal practices to integrate into your daily life.

Informal Practices

☐   Mindful Listening

☐   Loving-Kindness in Everyday Life

☐   RAIN

☐   Being Mindful of Habits

☐   Minding Your Pain

☐   STOP

☐   Bringing the Eight Attitudes of Mindfulness into Your Life

☐   Weaving Mindfulness Throughout Your Day

☐   Mindful Eating

Formal Practice Log

Each time you do a formal practice, fill out the following log. As you fill it out, and as you look back over the previous week's practice, think about how your practice has been going. Do you notice any patterns about what works best for you? What changes could you make to sustain the discipline?

Date and practice	Time	Thoughts, feelings, and sensations that arose during this practice and how you felt afterward

Reflecting on Informal Practice

Take some time every day to reflect on at least one instance of informal practice. You can use what you learn from these reflections to deepen your daily informal practice.

Practice	What was the situation?	What did you notice before?	What did you notice after?	What did you learn?

❈ chapter 10 ❈

the healthy path of mindful eating, exercise, rest, and connection

In past chapters you've explored various formal and informal practices of mindfulness and how they can help you cultivate greater ease, freedom, and peace, even when you face stress, anxiety, and pain. In this chapter, you'll learn how mindfulness is vital to living optimally physically, as well as mentally and emotionally. Human beings aren't sedentary creatures; we're mobile bipeds with bodies that need to be cared for. The human body needs proper food, exercise, and rest to maintain health and well-being. And because we're social creatures, connection with others is also important.

Bringing mindfulness to your lifestyle and physiological well-being is an important facet of reducing anxiety and stress. When experiencing stress and anxiety, you may have less energy to take care of yourself. Perhaps you've come to rely on various quick fixes to satisfy your immediate needs, such as unhealthy foods, poor eating habits, not exercising, not getting enough sleep, or not taking the time to connect with others. Though these strategies might help you cope in the short term, all will negatively impact your health and well-being and add to your stress and anxiety in the long run.

mindful eating revisited

We depend on food to survive. Only oxygen and water are more critical. Since preparing and eating food is such an essential component of our lives, why not bring mindful awareness to this? The processes of shopping for food and preparing food can be a wonderful focus for mindfulness. Really take in the colors, textures, and aromas of different foods. Notice their taste and texture at different points in the cooking process. Feel the utensils in your hands, hear the sizzle in a pan on the stove, and notice how disparate ingredients are transformed and melded together in the final dish. You might even bring loving-kindness to the process, preparing the food deliberately and with love, and with the wish that all who eat it will be suffused with health, well-being, and the love that went into preparing the food. Some people believe that the cook's energy is transferred into the food. Whether or not this is the case, what do you have to lose by taking this approach? If nothing else, it will help you grow in mindfulness.

If you're like most people, your mind is often somewhere else when you're eating, perhaps focused on the television, the computer, something you're reading, the conversation, memories, or thoughts and plans for the future. You may hardly notice the food you're placing in your mouth. As a result, you miss out on enjoying the food and may tend to overeat. Eating mindlessly or hurriedly can also cause physical problems. Many people who suffer from a sensitive stomach have learned that if they just chew their food longer and more slowly, they don't experience the intensity or frequency of discomfort.

Listen to your body to notice whether you're truly hungry or not, and if you are, be mindful of what foods you choose to eat. Be present to the chewing, tasting, and swallowing, and to when you've had enough to eat and it's time to stop. Also bring your awareness to when you may be inclined to eat for reasons other than hunger. If you're eating for emotional reasons, consider bringing mindful self-inquiry to the emotions, rather than soothing them or dulling yourself with food. If you're eating or drinking for a quick fix—for a boost of energy or to change your mind state or mood, once again consider mindful self-inquiry so that you can understand the situations and feelings that may fuel unhealthy habits. If you need energy, perhaps more rest is the answer.

At a more basic level, the body is continually rebuilding itself, and food provides both the fuel and the raw materials for this process. Looking at the situation this way underscores the old wisdom that you are what you eat—something to consider when you're about to opt for junk food or fast food. The body simply can't do as good of a job in building itself when you provide raw materials filled with artificial ingredients and empty calories. There are many philosophies about what constitutes the optimal diet, and it's worthwhile to look into this and consider the health impacts of the foods you eat. Furthermore, we're all different. Back in 1956, biochemist Roger Williams wrote a groundbreaking book entitled *Biochemical Individuality*, in which he put forth the idea that we are all unique, genetically and biochemically. As such, we differ in anatomy and metabolism, and in nutritional needs. Mindfulness can be extremely helpful in determining the diet that's best for you. As you continue to practice mindful eating, extend your awareness to how the food you eat impacts you. Do you feel better or worse after eating? Do you have more energy or less, and is that energy sustained or does it fizzle out quickly? Do certain foods create uncomfortable symptoms? These may extend beyond gastrointestinal symptoms. Perhaps certain foods make your heart race, make you feel dizzy, lead to a headache, and so on.

informal practice: Mindful Eating Revisited

In chapter 1, we introduced the formal practice of mindfully eating a raisin. In that practice, you noticed the full spectrum of sensory experiences associated with food—not just the flavor, but the appearance, the aroma, the texture, and even the sound. Now we'll extend that approach to bringing awareness and appreciation to all of the people and all of the processes involved in bringing food to your table. Before you take your first bite, think of the farmers, the truckers, and those who work in the grocery store. If you didn't cook the food yourself, extend your appreciation to the person who devoted time and love to preparing this food for you. You can further extend your appreciation to the sun, the soil, the water, and the air, which are all woven into the very essence of this food and provided the foundation for its existence and your own. There truly is grace in reflecting on food in this way before beginning to eat. We recommend that before you take your first bite, you devote a few moments to the following reflections inspired by Thich Nhat Hanh (Deer Park Monastery 2009):

- May I receive this food as a gift from the earth, the sky, and all the living beings and their hard work that made it possible for me to nourish this body and mind.

- May I eat with mindfulness and gratitude so as to be worthy to receive this food.

- May I recognize and transform my unhealthy habitual behaviors, especially my greed, and learn to eat with moderation.

- May I keep my compassion alive by eating in such a way that I reduce the suffering of living beings, preserve our planet, and help reverse the process of global warming.

- May I accept this food so that I may nurture my strength to be of service to others.

When you're ready, bring the first bite to your mouth, open your lips, and take the food into your mouth. Pay careful attention to what happens next. How does it feel in your mouth? Do thoughts, judgments, or stories arise? If so, gently acknowledge them then return the focus to the direct sensations unfolding as you begin to chew. Notice the taste. Is it sweet, sour, earthy, bitter, or something else? Is the texture smooth, crunchy, grainy, or chewy? Does the taste change as you continue chewing? Notice how that first mouthful eventually disappears, how swallowing happens. Just acknowledge this as it occurs and let it be.

Consider this humorous true story of Henry, a man who used to take a handful of raisins and shove them in his mouth all at once. This was how he had eaten them all his life. When he was introduced to the practice of mindful eating with a raisin, he noticed the curves and light shining in various areas of an individual raisin and how it made a squishy sound next to his ear. He also noticed that the raisin had a smell. All of this was very interesting to him. But when he put it in his mouth and started chewing it, something unexpected happened: He realized he wasn't enjoying the taste of the raisin. Although he had spent years shoving raisins in his mouth, mostly when he was feeling moody, eating mindfully led Henry to the insight that he had never really paid attention to the taste of raisins. In the end, Henry laughed at his discovery that he actually didn't even like raisins.

Everyone does this at times. It's amazing how unaware we can be of the food we take in. By bringing mindfulness to the food you eat, you can begin to choose foods that are more enjoyable and support your well-being, and know that you're taking care of yourself.

explore: Understanding Emotional Eating

When you were young, people may have offered you comfort foods when you were sick or unhappy. You may be filled with warm memories of Mom or Dad serving you a favorite food or snack. Now that you're an adult, when strong emotions arise, such as anger, sadness, anxiety, or confusion, you may turn to food for comfort. Reflect on how your moods interact with your eating patterns. Are there certain foods you turn to for comfort? Do you choose different foods depending on whether you're feeling angry, sad, anxious, or confused? Write about any connections you see between your moods and your eating patterns. Also reflect on whether you tend to eat in response to particular situations or interactions.

_____

_____

_____

_____

_____

_____

Just reflecting on how your mood might influence when and what you eat can make you more aware, in the moment, of when uncomfortable emotions trigger an urge to eat mindlessly or unhealthfully. In that moment, you can choose your response—and as Viktor Frankl suggested, in your response lies your growth and your freedom.

Before you move on, take a moment to compassionately reflect on, acknowledge, and integrate what you learned in this exploration.

mindful exercise

Human beings are dynamic organisms born to move. It's important to honor this aspect of your being by including exercise in your approach to working with stress and anxiety. In fact, physical exercise is one of the best stress relievers, decreasing the body's production of stress hormones and increasing levels of those feel-good neurotransmitters known as endorphins. Unless we overdo it, most of us feel better after a workout. Isn't it great that you can have fun with movement and that it's healthy for you? One simple golden rule is to move every day, and do so vigorously enough to work up a sweat. Sometimes there's a misconception that mindfulness means always doing things slowly. In truth, it simply means being aware. You can walk slowly or sprint quickly with mindfulness.

As mentioned earlier, *yoga* literally means "to yoke" or "to bring the mind and body together." Bringing mindfulness to any physical activity will definitely increase the benefits. Bodybuilder, movie star, and politician Arnold Schwarzenegger reportedly maintained that "a single, mindful repetition of an exercise—when he concentrated completely on the movement of a particular muscle—yielded infinitely better results than twenty reps where the future governor of California let his mind wander" (Moore and Stevens 2004, 34). You need not be as ripped as Arnold, or even aspire to be, to discover that by bringing mindfulness to exercise you can maximize the benefits of whatever activity you're doing and heed your body's wisdom about overdoing it or underdoing it.

Bring mindfulness to any exercise or movement activity just as you did with mindful walking and mindful yoga. You may discover that you enjoy yourself more when you're present to your body in movement.

---

informal practice: Mindful Exercise

In everyday life there are so many ways to move the body with awareness. You can choose from stretching, running, yoga, qigong, tai chi, swimming, snorkeling, water-skiing, scuba diving, ice-skating, hang gliding, bicycling, rowing, skiing, badminton, lacrosse, gymnastics, snowboarding, canoeing, Pilates, soccer, dancing, football, Ping-Pong, tennis, hockey, hiking, or working out at the gym or the house. There are literally thousands of ways to move and stay healthy. We would like you to practice any form of movement or exercise of your choice throughout the week. And don't overlook walking. It's simple, effective, and doesn't require any special equipment or entail any expense. Plus, you can do it almost anytime, anywhere.

---

explore: Working with Resistance to Exercise

Do you find it hard to get up and move? Do you resist exercising, even if you've set an intention to do so more often? What are the obstacles that get in your way? Reflect on what stops you from moving and take some time to explore anything that comes up in your body, thoughts, and emotions. Conversely, are there times or situations where you find it easier to exercise, or can you think of any strategies that might make it easier for you to get more active? Perhaps you'd enjoy exercising with a friend, or maybe you'd tend to follow through if you link exercise with another activity you already do.

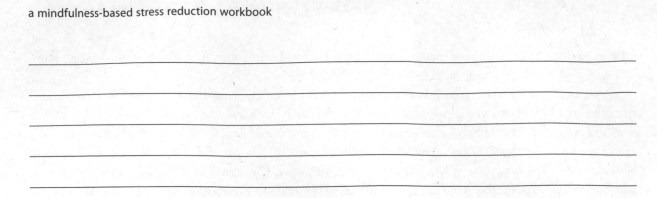

In working with exercise, it's sometimes helpful to ask how much exercise do you really think you can do? Whatever springs to mind, do a little bit less. The strategy behind this is to allow the mind to really believe it can do it and lessen the resistance.

Before you move on, take a moment to compassionately reflect on, acknowledge, and integrate what you learned in this exploration.

the gift of rest

Nature teaches us about balance. Each day brings light and each night brings darkness, and each functions in its own way to support the world. If there were only sunlight or only darkness, life wouldn't flourish. The wisdom of Ecclesiastes 3:1 applies here: "To everything there is a season, and a time to every purpose under heaven." Just as it's important to make time for movement, it's essential to find time for stillness.

It's important to ask yourself whether you may be doing too much. People new to meditation often say they frequently fall asleep when practicing. Sometimes avoidance is the reason, but in most cases the cause is fatigue. When you don't listen to the needs of the body, it's easy to lose touch with your own natural cycles of activity and rest. You can look at your meditation cushion and think you should be sitting on it to meditate, but deep down a wiser voice may be saying, "Wouldn't it be nice to put my head on it and sleep?" May you begin to listen to your deeper voice and rest when necessary. Perhaps after a good nap you'll be ready to meditate.

informal practice: The Gift of Rest

Use your daily schedule and calendar not just to plan activity, but to remind yourself to do nothing. Why not schedule "do nothing" just like you'd schedule a doctor's appointment? It's very healing to sometimes do nothing, go nowhere, and not have to be "on" for other people. Doing nothing can take many forms:

You can take a nap, go to bed earlier or get up later, sit in a chair, look out a window, be quiet, or lie down and put your feet up. Try turning off the telephone, radio, computer, stereo, and all of the endless other electronic devices and simply enjoy some time in solitude and nondoing. If you'd like to connect with nature more, plan to spend an afternoon outdoors, hanging out by the ocean, a lake, or a stream or in the desert, the mountains, a forest, or any quiet natural environment. Notice what happens when you take the time to just be in these settings. If you have children, see if you can get a babysitter so you, or you and your partner, can take some time to do nothing. You may be amazed, but the world won't fall apart if you take a break.

explore: Working with Resistance to Rest

Do you find it hard to stop and take time to relax? Do you resist relaxing even if you've set an intention to do so more often? Reflect on the obstacles that get in the way of stopping to rest. Take a moment to explore anything that comes up in your body, thoughts, and emotions. Conversely, are there times or situations where you find it easier to relax, or can you think of any strategies that might make it easier for you to do so more often? Perhaps you need to ask others to pitch in and help around the house, or maybe you need to encourage others to relax so that you can feel more comfortable taking some downtime.

_____

_____

_____

_____

_____

_____

Even though it seems antithetical to "do nothing" when our culture tells us to stay active and productive at all costs, allow yourself to think of this as a meaningful and productive activity to benefit your mental health. Sometimes taking a little time to relax in this way may be exactly what your mind and body are calling for.

Before you move on, take a moment to compassionately reflect on, acknowledge, and integrate what you learned in this exploration.

connection: we are not islands

Although we come into and go out of this world alone, most of us are social creatures, and we need one another to survive. Just look at the world we have created, with endless roads and communication devices to connect us, and countless group endeavors, from agriculture to education to science to technology and so much more. Human beings look to one another for support and interaction, and to learn, grow, and share with each other. And although the universe is vast, its expanses remain inaccessible, so at least for now it seems that one another and our fellow beings on this planet are all that we have.

One of the deepest and most satisfying qualities of well-being is to love and be loved, and in fact, a growing body of research indicates that love and connection are vital for physical health. Dr. Dean Ornish, the cardiologist who developed a landmark approach to reversing heart disease, wrote a book on the importance of loving connections, called *Love and Survival* (1999). In this pioneering book, he cites numerous studies showing that being loved, giving love, and connecting with others promote health and well-being and can even increase longevity and resilience from illness. In one interesting study, residents in a nursing home who had a pet or even a plant to care for lived longer than those who had nothing to look after. Other studies revealed that those who had meaningful relationships and felt their life had purpose lived longer, and most importantly, were happier than those who didn't. The same was true of those who gave back to their community or connected with some type of spirituality.

As you pursue your inner journey of mindfulness and meditation, you will forge a better connection with yourself, coming to see yourself with more understanding and compassion and getting more in touch with your purpose, your passions, and what makes life meaningful for you. This connection with yourself is an important starting point and a strong foundation for connecting with others more deeply and genuinely.

Understand that connection extends beyond our relationships with our fellow human beings. This is one of the gifts of the loving-kindness meditation you learned in chapter 8: It helps cultivate an expansive awareness and connection with all living beings, and indeed, all of the universe. And yet this meditation begins with you—with your heart, and with your place in the world. We all have a place in this world, and it's wonderful when we can rejoice in it. It's not necessary to be famous or do something the world calls great. Ambition and thirsting after achievement and recognition are endless and in the end feed pride and conceit, leading to great suffering. The way to find your purpose, and to find peace, is to look into your heart, as Saint Isaac of Nineveh gently invites us to do: "Be at peace with your own soul, then heaven and earth will be at peace with you. Enter eagerly into the treasure house that is within you, and you will see the things that are in heaven; for there is but one single entry to them both. The ladder that leads to the Kingdom is hidden within your soul… Dive into yourself, and in your soul you will discover the stairs by which to ascend" (Oman 2000, 251).

---

informal practice: Mindful Connection

Human beings are social animals, and the sweetness of relationships with others and the larger world—indeed, the universe—can nourish our lives. As you deepen your connections, you'll find increasing delight in this interplay of giving and receiving. It may even become mysterious as to who is actually giving and who is receiving.

There are many things you can do to foster connection. Try sincerely asking a family member, friend, or anyone at all how he or she is doing, and listen deeply to what the other person says. Everyone loves to be heard and understood—to "feel felt." Or practice random acts of kindness toward anyone, including strangers. You might volunteer to help a child, an elderly person, or anyone in need. You can offer time and energy to an organization that's helping make the world a better place, or simply enjoy a pet, grow a garden, or pick up litter. Feel the sweetness of connecting with the world and its beings without wanting or expecting anything from them.

Just Do It!

How connected do you feel to those around you? Are those you spend most of your time with supportive of you or not? Make a mental list or write down those who are supportive of you and find ways to increase your connection with them. You could call someone to make a date or just to talk. You could write a letter or an email to a loved one. You could ask a friend or family member to go for a walk with you, or you might make time to play with a child, take your dog for a walk, or pet your cat. Go ahead and do this now, or schedule in your calendar a date to *just do it!*

explore: Working with Resistance to Connection

Even though you may long for connection, sometimes you may feel inhibited or resistant. What holds you back from connecting with yourself, others, or the world? When you try to connect, do you notice fear? Do you notice that you make excuses to isolate yourself from others or from the larger world around you? Take a moment to explore anything that comes up in your body, thoughts, and emotions. Conversely, consider what you already do to connect or to deepen your connections. Are there ways you can build on these ways of connecting? How do you feel in your mind and body when you experience connection?

_____

_____

_____

_____

_____

_____

_____

One thing we know is that an important aspect of mental health is cultivating healthy relationships with others. However, sometimes our own walls and barriers get in the way of connection. May you know that even the act of taking the time to explore the process of connecting with others is a gift to yourself.

Before you move on, take a moment to compassionately reflect on, acknowledge, and integrate what you learned in this exploration.

FAQ

Is there more that I need to cultivate better living besides meditation, healthy eating, exercise, rest, and connection?

Sometimes you can be burdened by a tendency to think you need to do more in order to reach some better place—that whatever you're doing isn't enough. It's common for the mind to habitually strive to do more and more, and this can be a source of distress. However, the very moment you notice this habit you have become present and can choose to be mindful once again. Try on the attitude of nonstriving and simply engage with whatever practice for better living you're already engaged in. The Buddha spoke about seeing for yourself through your own direct experience what is true and what isn't. If you're living a healthy lifestyle, you'll know; and if you aren't, you'll know that too. Trust the wisdom of your own direct experience.

How Stressed Are You?

Congratulations on making it through chapter 10! Throughout your journey with this book, you've cultivated mindful living with a variety of formal and informal practices. Take a moment to thank yourself for allowing this gift of time. When you started reading this book, you listed your primary stressors at the end of the introduction on page 11 and rated the severity of the stress they caused. Halfway through the book, you reviewed and revised this list and rated your stressors once again. Before moving on to chapter 11, where you'll create a plan for continuing your practice of mindfulness, take a moment to revisit the stressors you wrote down at that time and assess how you're doing with them now.

Try to make this a mindful process. Before diving in with scoring, take a moment to breathe and check in with your body. Then take some time to think about each stressor and see if you feel differently or the same about it. If any new stressors have arisen, add them to the list and rate them as well.

Planning and Reviewing Your Practice

At this point, you can schedule any of the meditation practices you've learned in this workbook for at least five days this week. Go ahead and put them on your calendar over the next week or two. It's fine to mix them up throughout the week. Also schedule a time about a week from now when you'll review your practice to see how it's going.

Formal Practices

☐ Mindful Breathing

☐ Walking Meditation

☐ Body Scan

☐ Sitting Meditation

☐ Mindful Yoga

☐ Mindful Self-Inquiry for Stress and Anxiety

☐ Loving-Kindness Meditation

Now you have a wide variety of informal practices to incorporate into your day-to-day life.

Informal Practices

☐ Mindful Connection

☐ The Gift of Rest

☐ Mindful Exercise

☐ Mindful Listening

☐ Loving-Kindness in Everyday Life

☐ RAIN

☐ Being Mindful of Habits

☐ Minding Your Pain

☐ STOP

☐ Bringing the Eight Attitudes of Mindfulness into Your Life

☐ Weaving Mindfulness Throughout Your Day

☐ Mindful Eating

Formal Practice Log

Each time you do a formal practice, fill out the following log. As you fill it out, and as you look back over the previous week's practice, think about how your practice has been going. Do you notice any patterns about what works best for you? What changes could you make to sustain the discipline? At this point, you may wish to make several copies of the log so that you can use it to record and review your practice in the months to come.

Date and practice	Time	Thoughts, feelings, and sensations that arose during this practice and how you felt afterward

Reflecting on Informal Practice

Take some time every day to reflect on at least one instance of informal practice. You can use what you learn from these reflections to deepen your daily informal practice. As with the Formal Practice Log, you may wish to make photocopies of this blank form for future use.

Practice	What was the situation?	What did you notice before?	What did you notice after?	What did you learn?

❋ chapter 11 ❋

keeping up your practice

Congratulations on nearly completing this workbook. Though this may feel like an ending, it's really just one step forward into a new way of life. Mindfulness begins by paying close attention to whatever you experience in the here and now. It's an unfolding process—just experiencing life one moment and one breath at a time.

Throughout this book, you've learned a variety of formal and informal mindfulness practices, as well as ways of weaving mindfulness into all of the daily activities of your life. As you continue to practice, you'll cultivate deeper levels of insight and compassion and be able to play a more active and effective role in the management of your health and well-being. Paying attention to the present moment in day-to-day life plays a central role in this process. The sooner you can identify and be mindful of a stressful situation, the sooner you can disentangle yourself from typical reactions and mind traps. This will open the door to new possibilities and more skillful responses. The best way to foster this awareness is to continue to practice mindfulness, both formally and informally, as much as possible. Remember, mindfulness is always accessible, and in the very moment that you realize you aren't present, you've become present once again; it's that simple.

That said, a certain amount of organization and scheduling can ensure that you continue to practice and grow in mindfulness. Here are some suggestions for keeping your practice going both, formally and informally:

- **First month.** In the next few pages, we'll help you explore and plan your practice over the next month. You'll select formal and informal practices to focus on, schedule your practices, and schedule your review, just as you've been doing throughout your work with this book.

- **Beyond the first month.** After one month, feel free to rotate among the practices, choosing whichever practice speaks to you on any given day.

- **Workbook review.** When you feel ready, go through this workbook again with the attitude of beginner's mind. You're likely to discover new aspects of the practices or a new understanding of the material. Rereading this book would also be an excellent way to bolster your commitment to practice.

- **Community.** The importance of connecting with a like-minded and supportive community cannot be overemphasized. The Resources section offers some information that may be helpful in finding a local mindfulness meditation sitting group. Also consider joining the online mindfulness community focused on the contents of this workbook at www.mbsrworkbook.com.

explore: Creating Your Formal Way

Mindfulness is a personal journey, and some practices may resonate with you more than others. Read through the list of the formal practices you've learned in this book, then explore and compare your experiences with them. You may want to read through your old formal practice logs to help you decide which practices you'd like to emphasize.

Formal Practices

- Mindfully Eating a Raisin
- Mindful Check-In
- Mindful Breathing
- Walking Meditation
- Body Scan
- Sitting Meditation
- Mindful Lying Yoga
- Mindful Self-Inquiry for Stress and Anxiety
- Mindful Standing Yoga
- Loving-Kindness Meditation

_____

_____

_____

_____

_____

_____

_____

While mindfulness may seem to be simple, by now you understand that it's a practice that requires effort and discipline. It's all too easy to get caught up in well-worn grooves and fall back into running on autopilot. As you continue in your practice, may you have compassion for yourself when you realize that you've let time pass without practicing. Remember, in that very moment you are present once again. Choose to invite yourself to renew your practice.

setting up your formal practice

For the next month, each week choose two or three practices and schedule them on your calendar. It's fine to emphasize your favorite practices or those that come most easily, but occasionally choose others that are more challenging as a way to continue to deepen and expand your process. Also continue to schedule weekly reviews. This may help you commit more fully to your practice and will also provide feedback that will help you determine which practices are most effective for you and what rhythm best supports you in reducing anxiety and stress and building compassion. Go ahead and schedule your next week of practice now, before reading on.

explore: Creating Your Informal Way

In the same way that doing formal practice is a personal journey, you may have appreciated some informal practices more than others. Read through the list of informal practices you've learned in this book, then explore and compare your experiences with them. You may want to read through all of your reviews of informal practice to help you decide which you'd like to emphasize.

Informal Practices

- Mindful Eating

- Weaving Mindfulness Throughout Your Day

- Bringing the Eight Attitudes of Mindfulness into Your Life

- STOP

- Minding Your Pain

- Being Mindful of Habits

- RAIN

- Loving-Kindness in Daily Life

- Mindful Listening

- Mindful Eating Revisited

- Mindful Exercise

- The Gift of Rest

- Mindful Connection

_____

_____

_____

_____

_____

_____

_____

Opportunities to practice mindfulness are all around you. By integrating mindfulness into your daily life, you can break out of routine and find your way back into wonder. It can truly turn the seemingly ordinary into something extraordinary. As the late Richard Carlson suggested in his book *Don't Sweat the Small Stuff—And It's All Small Stuff* (1997), you'll find that you more naturally start to be grateful for the good times and graceful during the more difficult times. May you continue to remind yourself to bring mindfulness into all of the many facets of your life.

continuing your informal practice

Continue to weave the informal practices in this book into your day-to-day life, emphasizing those you resonate with and those that are most beneficial for you, as perhaps revealed by the preceding exploration. Use these as a basis for creating your own informal practices. Also, bear in mind that you can bring informal practice into any daily activity. Since we really live only in the present moment, why not be there for it as fully as possible? To do so, simply tune in to your senses and also be aware of any thoughts or emotions that arise. Here are some examples:

- If you're taking a bath, notice the temperature of the water and the feeling of the soap or suds. Be aware of the scents that surround you and any sounds that occur, like bubbles popping or water swishing. What do you see, in terms of colors, shapes, and textures? Do any thoughts, memories, or emotions arise? If so, just acknowledge them, let them be, and gently bring yourself back to the present moment of bathing.

- If you're listening to music, hear and feel the rhythm of the sounds as they rise, fall, and change. Also notice any physical sensations, thoughts, or emotions that arise in connection with the music.

- If you're with a friend, intentionally choose to listen mindfully. If your mind wanders, as it inevitably will, just acknowledge this, let it be, and gently bring it back to listening deeply.

Be aware that some activities can also do a great deal to alleviate stress. Notable examples include exercising, soaking in a warm tub, laughing, journaling, yoga, walking, and gardening. A complete list would be lengthy and it's also highly personalized. Golf may be relaxing for some and entirely unappealing to others. Some people may find music relaxing, whereas for others it may be disruptive. We suggest applying mindfulness to determining which activities help reduce or manage your stress and then emphasizing those. Then, if you bring mindfulness to these activities, you're likely to redouble the benefits. And as you may have guessed, we also recommend that you continue to mindfully reflect on your informal practice. This will also help maximize the benefits of your practice. In crafting your ongoing practice, consider any of the following activities as an opportunity to practice mindfulness:

- ☐ Soaking in the bathtub
- ☐ Collecting things (stamps, shells, and so on)
- ☐ Sorting through old items for recycling or donation
- ☐ Jogging or walking
- ☐ Listening to music
- ☐ Laughing
- ☐ Listening to others
- ☐ Reading
- ☐ Crafts (ceramics, woodwork, and so on)
- ☐ Spending an evening with good friends
- ☐ Planning a day's activities
- ☐ Going to the gym or doing aerobics
- ☐ Cooking, baking, or preparing food
- ☐ Repairing things around the house
- ☐ Working on a car or bicycle
- ☐ Noting the loving words or deeds of others
- ☐ Putting on or taking off clothes
- ☐ Noticing stillness the early morning or in the evening
- ☐ Taking care of plants or a garden
- ☐ Swimming
- ☐ Doodling
- ☐ Playing team sports
- ☐ Flying a kite

- ☐ Drinking early morning coffee or tea and reading the newspaper
- ☐ Knitting, sewing, crocheting, or quilting
- ☐ Shooting pool
- ☐ Dressing up
- ☐ Going to a museum or art gallery
- ☐ Doing crosswords or other puzzles
- ☐ Surfing the Internet
- ☐ Watching a candle or a fire
- ☐ Listening to the radio
- ☐ Going out to eat or out for coffee
- ☐ Getting or giving a massage
- ☐ Communicating "I love you"
- ☐ Skiing
- ☐ Canoeing or white-water rafting
- ☐ Bowling
- ☐ Dancing
- ☐ Watching fish in an aquarium
- ☐ Horseback riding
- ☐ Rock climbing
- ☐ Doing something you've never done before
- ☐ Doing jigsaw puzzles
- ☐ Playing with pets
- ☐ Rearranging furniture
- ☐ Going window-shopping

- ☐ Going to the bathroom
- ☐ Taking a shower
- ☐ Cleaning house
- ☐ Folding the laundry
- ☐ Having discussions with friends or family
- ☐ Riding a motorbike
- ☐ Making love
- ☐ Singing alone or with others
- ☐ Arranging flowers
- ☐ Going to the beach
- ☐ Noting positive thoughts
- ☐ Ice-skating, roller-skating, or roller-blading
- ☐ Going sailing
- ☐ Sketching, painting, or doing other art
- ☐ Doing embroidery or cross-stitching
- ☐ Lying down for a nap or just to rest
- ☐ Driving
- ☐ Birdwatching
- ☐ Flirting
- ☐ Playing a musical instrument
- ☐ Making a gift for someone
- ☐ Hiking or going for a brisk walk
- ☐ Writing
- ☐ Working
- ☐ Sightseeing

- ☐ Gardening
- ☐ Being in the beauty salon
- ☐ Playing tennis or other racquet sports
- ☐ Kissing
- ☐ Watching children or pets play
- ☐ Going to a play or a concert
- ☐ Daydreaming
- ☐ Listening to music
- ☐ Refinishing furniture
- ☐ Making a to-do list
- ☐ Bicycling
- ☐ Spending time in nature
- ☐ Eating healthful food
- ☐ Eating gooey, delicious, forbidden foods
- ☐ Taking photographs
- ☐ Going fishing
- ☐ Thinking about pleasant events
- ☐ Stargazing
- ☐ Being alone
- ☐ Writing in a journal
- ☐ Writing a letter or personal email
- ☐ Going on a picnic
- ☐ Having lunch with a friend
- ☐ Playing cards or other games
- ☐ Seeing or showing photos or slides
- ☐ Washing the dishes

FAQ

My practice is dwindling. How can I revitalize my commitment to meditation?

An important part of keeping your practice going is to remain aware of how much better you feel when you practice regularly. Beyond that, have self-compassion and remember, the moment you realize you aren't present, you are present and your practice begins again. It may also be helpful to reflect on the preciousness and fragility of life and ask yourself what you're waiting for. Are you living the life you want to be living? This attitude is beautifully encapsulated in the ancient Buddhist language, Pali, with the powerful word *samvega*, which expresses that when you realize death can come at any moment, you are catapulted into realizing the importance of practice. Take a moment right now and ask yourself what's most important to you. If you want to experience more freedom and peace, regular mindfulness practice is the key that unlocks the door.

deepening your practice

We encourage you to participate in a mindfulness meditation retreat from time to time. There are many possibilities, ranging in duration from a day to a weekend to a week, a month, or even longer. Although the everyday practice of mindfulness is key, a meditation retreat is a wonderful complement that can profoundly deepen your practice. Two wonderful meditation centers that offer retreats throughout the year are Spirit Rock, in Woodacre, California, and the Insight Meditation Society, in Barre, Massachusetts. See the Resources section for contact information for these organizations.

closing words

Within a daily practice of mindfulness, you can more quickly discover when you're getting stressed, and thus return to balance more quickly. If the day is extremely challenging, even one minute of mindfulness can bring greater stillness. Also bear in mind that if you're often off somewhere else in the future or the past, you'll miss so many wonderful moments in everyday life. Remember, the main point is to be here and now, since this is where, and when, life is lived.

Our wish for you is that you develop a sense of balance and make the practice of mindfulness your own. Remember Viktor Frankl's words: "Between stimulus and response there is a space. In that space is our power to choose our response. In our response lies our growth and our freedom" (Pattakos 2008, viii).

May you remember to practice compassion
for yourself, all living beings, and the universe.
May all beings be at peace.

afterword

Here on Earth, 1.8 people die every second. That's 108 deaths per minute, 150,000 deaths per day, 55 million deaths per year. No amount of mindfulness or stress reduction is going to keep you and me from someday joining this inevitability. Yet dwelling for a time in the sobering reverberation of these numbers, this fact remains: today, right now, in this very moment, you and I are alive! This is a big deal. Often enough we take it for granted or simply forget.

A Mindfulness-Based Stress Reduction Workbook has been a reminder. Over and over again, Bob Stahl and Elisha Goldstein have asked us to remember the fundamental reality of being alive. They have invited us into seeing and hearing, touching and tasting, smelling and perceiving every instance of this one life that is ours to live—this one "wild and precious life" Mary Oliver calls us to remember, that Derek Walcott reminds us to "feast on," this one life, in all its unity and multiplicity that endlessly conspires to remind us of our fundamental wakefulness and innate human resourcefulness.

Reminding us of these things, this book has become our good fortune. More so because it is rooted in experience, it has provided us with a method that has the power and potential to carry us far beyond the completion of the last page. In practicing with this book, you've probably discovered that the work of awareness is never done. I hope that you've become captivated and compelled by the adventure of mindfulness. This workbook is a worthwhile traveling companion. We can explore and integrate its lessons for a long, long time because it has offered us a well-researched approach for learning to be more fully alive to ourselves, to the people who share our lives, and to the wonder and beauty of the world in all its light and darkness.

This book is like a wide field of acceptance offering us plenty of room to roam as we learn to become mercifully attentive to our reactive habits and conditioned states of mind and body. Such openness encourages clear seeing, the emergence of honesty, and an embodied ability to respond more skillfully to the challenges of living. Bob and Elisha have been spacious and precise with us. They trust our depth and breadth. In so doing, they encourage us to discover for ourselves Victor Frankl's insight:

> *Between stimulus and response there is a space.*
> *In that space is our power to choose our response.*
> *In our response lies our growth and our freedom.*

In a thousand ways, this book points to that space. Our work is now before us.

—Saki F. Santorelli, Ed.D., MA
Associate Professor of Medicine
Director, Stress Reduction Clinic
Executive Director, Center for Mindfulness in Medicine, Health Care, and Society
University of Massachusetts Medical School
Worcester, Massachusetts

resources

mindfulness audio

Mindfulness Meditation CDs by Bob Stahl

To purchase or listen to a sample of these CDs, visit www.mbsrworkbook.com or www.mindfulness programs.com/mindful-healing-series.html. You can also purchase them at Amazon.com.

- *Opening to Change, Forgiveness, and Loving-Kindness*
- *Working with Chronic Pain*
- *Working with Neck and Shoulder Pain*
- *Working with Back Pain*
- *Working with Insomnia and Sleep Challenges*
- *Working with Anxiety, Fear, and Panic*
- *Working with High Blood Pressure*
- *Working with Heart Disease*
- *Working with Headaches and Migraines*
- *Working with Asthma, COPD, and Respiratory Challenges*
- *Body Scan and Sitting Meditation*
- *Lying and Standing Yoga*
- *Impermanence and Loving-Kindness Meditation*

Mindfulness DVD by Bob Stahl, Ph.D.

- *Mindful Qigong and Loving-Kindness Meditation*

Mindful Solutions CDs by Elisha Goldstein, Ph.D.

For more information or to purchase these CDs, visit www.mbsrworkbook.com, elishagoldstein .com, or drsgoldstein.com. You can also purchase them at www.amazon.com.

- *Mindful Solutions for Stress, Anxiety, and Depression*

- *Mindful Solutions for Addiction and Relapse Prevention* (coauthored with Stefanie Goldstein, Ph.D.)

- *Mindful Solutions for Success and Stress Reduction at Work*

- *Mindful Solutions for Adults with ADD/ADHD* (by Lidia Zylowska, MD)

mindfulness resources

Mindfulness-Based Stress-Reduction Programs

Mindfulness-Based Stress Reduction programs abound throughout the United States as well as internationally. If you're interested in joining a program near you, check out the regional and international directory at the Center for Mindfulness at University of Massachusetts Medical School's website: www.umassmed.edu/cfm/mbsr.

Mindfulness Meditation Centers and Weekly Sitting Groups

To find mindfulness meditation centers and weekly sitting groups in the United States, consult the following websites, which also offer lists of international meditation centers:

- For the West Coast, www.spiritrock.org

- For the East Coast, www.dharma.org

Online Mindfulness Programs

- If you're interested in joining a live online community focused on the content in this workbook, go to www.mbsrworkbook.com.

- If you would like to participate in a self-directed, multimedia, and interactive "Mindfulness, Anxiety, and Stress Program," by Bob Stahl and Elisha Goldstein, please go to: www.aliveworld.com/shops/mh1/mindfulness-Anxiety-and-Stress.aspx.

- If you can't find a local MBSR program or meditation center or group, consider participating in an online mindfulness-based stress reduction program with Steve Flowers: steve@mindfullivingprograms.com or www.mindfullivingprograms.com.

- Online Mindfulness Classes: www.emindful.com

Mindfulness Websites

- A *Mindfulness-Based Stress Reduction Workbook* website: www.mbsrworkbook.com

- Bob Stahl's website: www.mindfulnessprograms.com

- Elisha Goldstein's websites: www.drsgoldstein.com, www.elishagoldstein.com

- Center for Mindfulness at University of Massachusetts Medical School website: www .umassmed.edu/cfm

- Mind and Life Institute website: www.mindandlife.org

- Mindful Awareness Research Center (MARC) website: marc.ucla.edu

- Mindsight Institute website: www.mindsightinstitute.com

- www.mindfulnesstogether.com

- Insight LA website: www.insightla.org

- eMindful website: www.emindful.com

organizations and internet resources for stress and anxiety

Anxiety Disorders Association of America
    www.adaa.org
    The mission of this nonprofit organization is to promote the prevention, treatment, and cure of anxiety disorders and to improve the lives of all people who suffer from them.

The Anxiety Panic Internet Resource
    www.algy.com/anxiety
    This web-based resource offers forums and good information on anxiety and panic.

Obsessive-Compulsive Foundation
    www.ocfoundation.org
    This is the top website for thorough information on obsessive compulsive disorder.

additional reading

Mindfulness Meditation

Analayo, B. 2002. *Satipatthana: The Direct Path to Realization*. Birmington, UK: Windhorse.

Bodhi, B. 1994. *The Noble Eightfold Path: The Way to the End of Suffering*. Kandy, Sri Lanka: Buddhist Publication Society.

Boorstein, S. 1997. *It's Easier Than You Think: The Buddhist Way to Happiness*. San Francisco: HarperOne.

Brach, T. 2004. *Radical Acceptance*. New York: Bantam.

Chödrön, P. 2000. *When Things Fall Apart.* Boston: Shambhala.

———. 2007. *The Places That Scare You.* Boston: Shambhala.

Dass, R., and S. Levine. 1988. *Grist for the Mill.* Berkeley, CA: Celestial Arts.

Epstein, M. 1995. *Thoughts Without a Thinker.* New York: Perseus Group.

———. 2001. *Going on Being: Life at the Crossroads of Buddhism and Psychotherapy.* New York: Broadway Books.

Goldstein, J. 1983. *The Experience of Insight.* Boston: Shambhala.

———. 2003. *Insight Meditation: The Practice of Freedom.* Boston: Shambhala.

———. 2003. *One Dharma: The Emerging Western Buddhism.* San Francisco: Harper.

Goldstein, J., and J. Kornfield. 2001. *Seeking the Heart of Wisdom.* Boston: Shambhala.

Gunaratana, B. H. 2002. *Mindfulness in Plain English.* Boston: Wisdom.

Kabat-Zinn, J. 1990. *Full Catastrophe Living.* New York: Delta.

———. 1994. *Wherever You Go, There You Are.* New York: Hyperion.

———. 2005. *Coming to Our Senses.* New York: Hyperion.

———. 2007. *Arriving at Your Own Door: 108 Lessons in Mindfulness.* New York: Hyperion.

Kornfield, J. 1993. *A Path with Heart.* New York: Bantam.

———. 2000. *After the Ecstasy, the Laundry.* New York: Bantam.

———. 2008. *The Wise Heart.* New York: Bantam.

Levine, N. 2003. *Dharma Punx.* San Francisco: Harper Collins.

———. 2007. *Against the Stream.* San Francisco: Harper Collins.

Levine, S. 1989. *A Gradual Awakening.* New York: Anchor.

Nhat Hanh, T. 1996. *The Miracle of Mindfulness.* Boston: Beacon.

———. 2005. *Being Peace.* Berkeley, CA: Parallax Press.

Rahula, W. 1974. *What the Buddha Taught.* New York: Grove Press.

Rosenberg, L. 1998. *Breath by Breath: The Liberating Practice of Insight Meditation.* Boston: Shambhala.

———. 2000. *Living in the Light of Death.* Boston: Shambhala.

Salzberg, S. 1997. *A Heart as Wide as the World.* Boston: Shambhala.

———. 2002. *Lovingkindness.* Boston: Shambhala.

Sayadaw, M. L. 1965. *Manual of Insight*, translated by S. U. Nyana. Rangoon, Burma: Union Buddha Sasana Council. Available at www.dhammaweb.net/html/view.php?id=2.

Sumedho, A. 1995. *The Mind and the Way*. Boston: Wisdom.

———. 2007. *The Sound of Silence*. Boston: Wisdom.

Thera, Narada. 1977. *The Buddha and His Teachings*. Kuala Lumpur, Malaysia: Buddhist Missionary Society.

Thera, Nyanaponika. 1973. *The Heart of Buddhist Meditation*. Boston: Weiser Books.

Thera, Nyanatilkoa. 1959. *The Word of the Buddha*. Kandy, Sri Lanka: Buddhist Publication Society.

Thera, P. 1979. *The Buddha's Ancient Path*. Kandy, Sri Lanka: Buddhist Publication Society.

Thomas, C. A. 2006. *At Hell's Gate: A Soldier's Journey*. Boston: Shambhala.

Trungpa, C. 2002. *Cutting Through Spiritual Materialism*. Boston: Shambhala.

———. 2002. *The Myth of Freedom*. Boston: Shambhala.

Stress, Illness, and Healing

Bennett-Goleman, T. 2001. *Emotional Alchemy*. New York: Three Rivers Press.

Benson, H. 1976. *The Relaxation Response*. New York: Harper.

Bourne, E. J. 2005. *The Anxiety and Phobia Workbook*, 4th edition. Oakland, CA: New Harbinger.

Brantley, J. 2007. *Calming Your Anxious Mind: How Mindfulness and Compassion Can Free You from Anxiety, Fear, and Panic*. Oakland, CA: New Harbinger.

Chödrön, P. 1997. *When Things Fall Apart*. Boston: Shambhala.

Chopra, D. 1988. *Quantum Healing: Exploring the Frontiers of Mind/Body Medicine*. New York: Bantam.

Cousins, N. 2005. *Anatomy of an Illness*. New York: W. W. Norton.

Flowers, S. 2009. *Mindful Path Through Shyness*. Oakland, CA: New Harbinger.

Frankl, V. 2000. *Man's Search for Meaning*. Boston: Beacon Press.

Levine, S. 1989. *Healing Into Life and Death*. New York: Anchor.

Moyers, B. 1995. *Healing and the Mind*. New York: Main Street Books.

Muller, W. 1999. *Sabbath: Restoring the Sacred Rhythm of Rest*. New York: Bantam.

Ornish, D. 1983. *Stress, Diet, and Your Heart*. New York: Henry Holt.

———. 1995. *Dr. Dean Ornish's Program for Reversing Heart Disease*. New York: Ballantine Books.

———. 1998. *Love and Survival*. New York: Harper Collins.

Remen, R. N. 1996. *Kitchen Table Wisdom*. New York: Riverhead Books.

———. 2000. *My Grandfather's Blessings*. New York: Riverhead Books.

Robbins, J. 1987. *Diet for a New America*. Tiburon, CA: H. J. Kramer.

———. 2006. *Healthy at 100*. New York: Random House.

Santorelli, S. 1999. *Heal Thyself: Lessons in Mindfulness in Medicine*. New York: Three Rivers Press.

Segal, Z., M. Williams, and J. Teasdale. 2002. *Mindfulness-Based Cognitive Therapy for Depression: A New Approach to Preventing Relapse*. New York: Guilford Press.

Selye, H. 1975. *Stress Without Distress*. New York: Signet.

———. 1978. *The Stress of Life*. New York: McGraw-Hill.

Shapiro, S., and L. Carlson. 2009. *The Art and Science of Mindfulness: Integrating Mindfulness into Psychology and the Helping Professions*. Washington DC: APA Books.

Siegel, D. 2007. *The Mindful Brain*. New York: W. W. Norton.

Weil, A. 2000. *Eating Well for Optimum Health*. New York: Alfred A. Knopf.

———. 2000. *Spontaneous Healing*. New York: Ballantine.

———. 2007. *Healthy Aging: A Lifelong Guide to Your Well-Being*. New York: Anchor.

Williams, M., J. Teasdale, Z. Segal, and J. Kabat-Zinn. 2007. *The Mindful Way Through Depression*. New York: Guilford Press.

Mindful Movement

Boccio, F. J. 2004. *Mindfulness Yoga*. Boston: Wisdom.

Cohen, K. 1997. *The Way of Qigong*. New York: Ballantine Books.

Conrad, E. 1997. *Life on Land: The Story of Continuum, the World-Renowned Self-Discovery and Movement Method*. Berkeley, CA: North Atlantic Books.

Feldenkrais, M. 1972. *Awareness Through Movement*. New York: Harper Collins.

Gintis, B. 2007. *Engaging the Movement of Life*. Berkeley, CA: North Atlantic Books.

Hu, B. 2004. *Wild Goose Qigong*. DVD. Berkeley, CA: Three Geese Productions.

Iyengar, B. K. 1992. *Light on Yoga*. New York: Schocken Books.

Lasater, J. H. 2000. *Living Your Yoga*. Berkeley, CA: Rodmell Press.

Poetry

Berry, W. 1998. *The Selected Poems of Wendell Berry*. Washington, DC: Perseus.

Eliot, T. S. 1963. *Collected Poems*. Orlando, FL: Harcourt Brace.

Emerson, R. W. 1994. *Ralph Waldo Emerson, Collected Poems and Translations*. New York: Penguin.

Hafiz. 1999. *The Gift*, translated by D. Ladinski. New York: Penguin.

Kabir. 2004. *Kabir: Ecstatic Poems*, translated by R. Bly. Boston: Beacon.

Kinnell, G. 2000. *A New Selected Poems*. New York: Houghton Mifflin.

Lao-tzu. 1944. *The Way of Life*, translated by W. Bynner. New York: Penguin.

Nelson, P. 1993. *There's a Hole in My Sidewalk: The Romance of Self-Discovery*. Hillsboro, OR: Beyond Words.

Oliver, M. 1992. *New and Selected Poems*. Boston: Beacon Books.

Rilke, R. M. 2000. *Letters to a Young Poet*, translated by J. Burnham. Novato, CA: New World Library.

Rumi. 2001. *The Soul of Rumi*, translated by C. Barks. San Francisco: Harper.

Ryokan. 1977. *One Robe, One Bowl*, translated by J. Stevens. New York: John Weatherhill.

Stafford, W. 1998. *The Way It Is*. St. Paul, MN: Graywolf Press.

Walcott, D. 1987. *Collected Poems*. New York: Farrar, Straus and Giroux.

Welwood, J. P. 1998. *Poems for the Path*. Mill Valley, CA: Jennifer Paine Welwood.

Whyte, D. 1994. *The Heart Aroused*. New York: Bantam Doubleday.

references

Ainsworth, M. D. S., M. C. Blehar, E. Waters, and S. Wall. 1978. *Patterns of Attachment: A Psychological Study of the Strange Situation.* Hillsdale, NJ: Erlbaum.

American Institute of Stress. 2009. Job stress. www.stress.org/job.htm. Accessed June 16, 2009.

American Psychological Association. 2004. The American Psychological Association recognizes ten companies' commitment to employee health and well-being. Press release, October 13. www.apa. org/releases/healthy.html. Accessed July 18, 2009.

Augustine. 2002. *The Confessions of St. Augustine,* trans. by A. C. Outler. Mineola, NY: Dover Publications.

Bastian, E. W., and T. L. Staley. 2009. *Living Fully, Dying Well: Reflecting on Death to Find Your Life's Meaning.* Boulder, CO: Sounds True.

Baxter, L. R., J. M. Schwartz, K. S. Bergman, M. P. Szuba, B. H. Guze, J. C. Mazziota, et al. 1992. Caudate glucose metabolic rate changes with both drug and behavior therapy for obsessive-compulsive disorder. *Archives of General Psychiatry* 49(9):681-689.

Benson, H. 1976. *The Relaxation Response.* New York: Harper.

Bohm, D. 1951. *Quantum Theory.* New York: Prentice Hall.

Bowlby, J. 1969. *Attachment and Loss.* Vol. 1, *Attachment.* New York: Basic Books and Hogarth Press.

Brefczynski-Lewis, J. A., A. Lutz, H. S. Schaefer, D. B. Levinson, and R. J. Davidson. 2007. Neural correlates of attentional expertise in long-term meditation practitioners. *Proceedings of the National Academy of Sciences* 104(27):11483-11488.

Brown, K., and R. Ryan. 2003. The benefits of being present: Mindfulness and its role in psychological well-being. *Journal of Personality and Social Psychology* 84(4):822-848.

Carlson, L., M. Speca, P. Faris, and K. Patel. 2007. One year pre-post intervention follow-up of psychological, immune, endocrine and blood pressure outcomes of mindfulness-based stress reduction (MBSR) in breast and prostate cancer outpatients. *Brain, Behavior, and Immunity* 21(8):1038-1049.

Carlson, R. 1997. *Don't Sweat the Small Stuff—And It's All Small Stuff.* New York: Hyperion.

Carson, J. W., K. M. Carson, K. M. Gil, and D. H. Baucom. 2006. Mindfulness-based relationship enhancement (MBRE) in couples. In *Mindfulness-Based Treatment Approaches*, edited by R. A. Baer. Burlington, MA: Academic Press.

Davidson, R. J., J. Kabat-Zinn, J. Schumacher, M. Rosenkranz, D. Muller, S. F. Santorelli, F. Urbanowski, A. Harrington, K. Bonus, and J. F. Sheridan. 2003. Alterations in brain and immune function produced by mindfulness meditation. *Psychosomatic Medicine* 65(4):564-570.

Deer Park Monastery. 2009. Eating meditation. www.deerparkmonastery.org/mindfulness-practice/eating-meditation. Accessed July 18, 2009.

Einstein, A. 1972. Letter quoted in the *New York Post.* November 28, p. 12.

Fisher, N. 2002. *Opening to You: Zen-Inspired Translations of the Psalms.* New York: Viking Compass.

Goldstein, J. 2003. *One Dharma: The Emerging Western Buddhism.* San Francisco: Harper.

Habington, W. 1634 [1895]. To my honoured friend Sir Ed. P. Knight. In *Castara.* London: A. Constable and Co.

Hanna, J. L. 2006. *Dancing for Health: Conquering and Preventing Stress.* Lanham, MD: AltaMira.

Heschel, A. J. 1955. *God in Search of Man: A Philosophy of Judaism.* New York: Farrar, Straus, Giroux.

Jarski, R. 2007. *Words from the Wise.* New York: Skyhorse Publishing.

Joyce, J. 2006. *Dubliners.* Clayton, DE: Prestwick House.

Kabat-Zinn, J. 1982. An outpatient program in behavioral medicine for chronic pain patients based on the practices of mindfulness meditation: Theoretical considerations and preliminary results. *General Hospital Psychiatry* 4(1):33-47.

Kabat-Zinn, J. 1990. *Full Catastrophe Living: Using the Wisdom of Your Body and Mind to Face Stress, Pain, and Illness.* New York: Delacourt.

Kabat-Zinn, J., A. Chapman, and P. Salmon. 1987. Relationship of cognitive and somatic components of anxiety to patient preference for different relaxation techniques. *Mind/Body Medicine* 2(3):101-110.

Kabat-Zinn, J., L. Lipworth, R. Burney, and W. Sellers. 1986. Four-year follow-up of a meditation-based program for the self-regulation of chronic pain: Treatment outcomes and compliance. *Clinical Journal of Pain* 2(3):159-173.

Kabat-Zinn, J., A. O. Massion, J. Kristeller, L. G. Peterson, K. Fletcher, L. Pbert, W. Linderking, and S. F. Santorelli. 1992. Effectiveness of a meditation-based stress reduction program in the treatment of anxiety disorders. *American journal of Psychiatry* 149(7):936-943.

Kabat-Zinn, J., E. Wheeler, T. Light, A. Skillings, M. Scharf, T. Cropley, D. Hosmer, and J. Bernhard. 1998. Influence of a mindfulness meditation-based stress reduction intervention on rates of skin clearing in patients with moderate to severe psoriasis undergoing phototherapy (UVB) and photo-chemotherapy (PUVA). *Psychosomatic Medicine* 60(5):625-632.

Kafka, F. 1946. *The Great Wall of China and Other Pieces.* London: Secker and Warburg.

King, M. L., Jr. 1981. *Strength to Love.* Philadelphia, PA: Fortress Press.

Lao-tzu. 1944. *The Way of Life According to Laotzu,* translated by W. Bynner. New York: John Day Company.

Lazar, S. W., C. E. Kerr, R. H. Wasserman, J. R. Gray, D. N. Greve, M. T. Treadway, et al. 2005. Meditation experience is associated with increased cortical thickness. *NeuroReport* 16(17):1893-1897.

Levey, J., and M. Levey. 2009. *Luminous Mind: Meditation and Mind Fitness.* San Francisco: Red Wheel.

Levine, S. 1987. *Healing Into Life and Death.* New York: Anchor Books.

Lewis, M. D., and R. M. Todd. 2005. Getting emotional: A neural perspective on emotion, intention, and consciousness. *Journal of Consciousness Studies* 12(8-10):210-235.

Lutz, A., J. Brefczynski-Lewis, T. Johnstone, and R. J. Davidson. 2008. Regulation of the neural circuitry of emotion by compassion meditation: Effects of meditative expertise. *PLoS One* 3(3):e1897.

Main, M., and R. Goldwyn. 1998. Adult attachment classification system. Unpublished manuscript. University of California, Berkeley.

Main, M., and J. Solomon. 1986. Discovery of an insecure-disorganized/disoriented attachment pattern. In T. B. Brazelton and M. W. Yogman, eds., *Affective Development in Infancy.* Norwood, NJ: Ablex Publishing.

Miller, J. J., K. Fletcher, and J. Kabat-Zinn. 1995. Three-year follow up and clinical implications of a mindfulness meditation-based stress reduction intervention in the treatment of anxiety disorders. *General Hospital Psychiatry* 17(3):192-200.

Moore, E., and K. Stevens. 2004. *Good Books Lately.* New York: Macmillan.

National Institute of Mental Health. 2008. The numbers count: Mental disorders in America. www.nimh.nih.gov/health/publications/the-numbers-count-mental-disorders-in-america/index.shtml#Intro. Accessed June 16, 2009.

Nelson, P. 1993. *There's a Hole in My Sidewalk: The Romance of Self-Discovery.* Hillsboro, OR: Beyond Words.

Nhat Hahn, T. 2001. *Anger: Wisdom for Cooling the Flames*. New York: Berkley Publishing.

Nhat Hanh, T. 2003. *Creating True Peace: Ending Violence in Yourself, Your Family, Your Community, and the World*. New York: Simon and Schuster.

Oliver, M. 1992. *New and Selected Poems*. Boston: Beacon Books.

Oman, M. (ed). 2000. *Prayers for Healing: 365 Blessings, Poems, and Meditations from Around the World*. Berkeley, CA: Conari Press.

Ornish, D. 1999. *Love and Survival: Eight Pathways to Intimacy and Health*. New York: HarperPerennial.

Parks, G. A., B. K. Anderson, and G. A. Marlatt. 2001. *Interpersonal Handbook of Alcohol Dependence and Problems*. New York: John Wiley.

Pattakos, A. 2008. *Prisoners of Our Thoughts: Viktor Frankl's Principles for Discovering Meaning in Life and Work*. San Francisco: Berrett-Koehler.

Powell, T. J., and S. Enright 1990. *Anxiety and Stress Management*. London: Routledge.

Rahula, W. 1974. *What the Buddha Taught*. New York: Grove Press.

Schore, A. 2003. *Affect Dysregulation and Disorders of the Self*. New York: W. W. Norton.

Segal, Z. V., J. M. G. Williams, J. D. Teasdale, and J. Kabat-Zinn. 2007. *The Mindful Way Through Depression*. New York: Guilford Press.

Shapiro, S., G. Schwartz, and G. Bonner. 1998. Effects of mindfulness-based stress reduction on medical and premedical students. *Journal of Behavioral Medicine* 21(6):581-589.

Shaver, P., and M. Mikulincer. 2002. Attachment-related psychodynamics. *Attachment and Human Development* 4(2):133-161.

Siegel, D. J. 2001. *The Developing Mind: How Relationships and the Brain Interact to Shape Who We Are*. New York: Guilford Press.

Siegel, D. J. 2007. *The Mindful Brain: Reflection and Attunement in the Cultivation of Well-Being*. New York: W. W. Norton.

Siegel, D. J. 2009. *Mindsight: The New Science of Personal Transformation*. New York: Bantam.

Thera, N. (translator). 2004. *The Dhammapada*. Whitefish, MT: Kessinger Publications.

Van Ijzendoorn, M. 1995. Adult attachment representations, parental responsiveness, and infant attachment: A meta-analysis on the predictive validity of the Adult Attachment Interview. *Psychological Bulletin* 117(3):387-403.

Walcott, D. 1976. *Sea Grapes*. London: Cape.

Welwood, J. P. 1998. *Poems for the Path*. Mill Valley, CA: Jennifer Paine Welwood.

Williams, R. J. 1956. *Biochemical Individuality*. New York: John Wiley and Sons.

Bob Stahl, Ph.D., founded and directs mindfulness-based stress reduction (MBSR) programs in three medical centers in the San Francisco Bay Area. A longtime mindfulness practitioner, he has completed MBSR teacher certification at University of Massachusetts Medical Center and lived in a Buddhist monastery for more than eight years. Bob also serves as adjunct senior teacher for Oasis, the institute for mindfulness-based professional education at the Center for Mindfulness in Medicine, Health Care, and Society at the University of Massachusetts Medical School.

Elisha Goldstein, Ph.D., is a clinical psychologist and cofounder of the Mindfulness Center for Psychotherapy and Psychiatry. He teaches MBSR and mindfulness-based cognitive therapy (MBCT) in West Los Angeles. He is author of the audio CD series *Mindful Solutions*, which deals with issues such as stress, anxiety, depression, addiction, adult ADHD, and success at work. He is also author of popular mindfulness and psychotherapy blogs on www. psychcentral.com and www.mentalhelp.net, and conducts workshops, radio interviews, and lectures on the therapeutic benefits of mindfulness.

© Gilles Mingasson

Foreword writer **Jon Kabat-Zinn, Ph.D.,** is author of numerous books, including *Full Catastrophe Living*; *Wherever You Go, There You Are*; and *Coming to Our Senses*.

Afterword writer **Saki Santorelli, Ed.D., MA**, is executive director of the Center for Mindfulness in Medicine, Health Care, and Society at the University of Massachusetts Medical School and author of *Heal Thyself*.

Visit www.mbsrworkbook.com for more information.

guided meditations

The disc included with this book contains twenty-one guided meditations, which all together comprise more than eight hours of audio programming. These meditations are in the MP3 audio format. Choosing this format made it possible for us to offer you a lot of audio content while conserving resources by including just one disc in the book. This disc will play on all MP3-compatible devices, which includes all personal computers and many home and car CD players. In order to use the disc, please choose one of the following:

MP3-Compatible CD or DVD Player

If you have a CD or DVD player in your home or car that displays the MP3 logo, your disc should play normally in that device. This is increasingly common, but not all devices support MP3. Even if your car player does support MP3, we caution you not to listen to these meditations while operating your vehicle.

Personal Computer

You can listen to this disc on a personal computer. Media player applications vary between systems, but most widely used applications, such as iTunes and Windows Media Player, will play MP3s. Insert the disc into your computer's optical drive. In most cases, your media player will launch automatically, and you'll be able to select the tracks you want to hear. If your application doesn't launch automatically, you should be able to open your media player and navigate to the track you want to hear through the application's file menu.

Portable Music Player

Using your media player application, you may transfer these tracks onto a portable music player such an iPod or a Zune. Please refer to the manufacturer's instructions for loading music onto your particular device.

For technical support, please call New Harbinger Publications at (800) 748-6273 (USA only) or (510) 652-0215.

TRACK LIST

1. Mindful Raisin Eating (5:19) with Elisha Goldstein
2. Mindful Check-In (3:54) with Elisha Goldstein
3. Mindful Breathing (5:36) with Elisha Goldstein
4. Mindful Breathing (15:21) with Elisha Goldstein
5. Mindful Walking Meditation (10:27) With Elisha Goldstein
6. Body Scan Meditation (15:56) with Bob Stahl
7. Body Scan Meditation (31:59) with Bob Stahl
8. Body Scan Meditation (45:29) with Bob Stahl
9. Sitting Meditation (15:33) with Bob Stahl
10. Sitting Meditation (30:24) with Bob Stahl
11. Sitting Meditation (45:35) with Bob Stahl
12. Mindful Yoga Introduction (1:33) with Bob Stahl
13. Mindful Lying Yoga (15:59) with Bob Stahl
14. Mindful Lying Yoga (31:17) with Bob Stahl
15. Mindful Lying Yoga (44:38) with Bob Stahl
16. Meditation on Anxiety and Stress (30:02) with Bob Stahl
17. Mindful Standing Yoga (16:20) with Bob Stahl
18. Mindful Standing Yoga (31:15) with Bob Stahl
19. Mindful Standing Yoga (45:31) with Bob Stahl
20. Loving-kindness Meditation (15:38) with Bob Stahl
21. Loving-kindness Meditation (33:59) with Bob Stahl
22. Loving-kindness Meditation (43:48) with Bob Stahl

index

mindfulness meditation: CD/DVD resources on, 201-202; centers and sitting groups, 203; concentration meditation vs., 8; deepening your practice of, 83, 198; emotions experienced in, 61; finding time for, 44; formal practice of, 87-89; habitual patterns and, 108; positions and posture for, 22, 44; practice suggestions for, 8-9; published resources on, 204-206; revitalizing your commitment to, 198; scheduling your practice of, 7, 23; sitting practice and, 83-90; sleepiness in, 45, 182; walking as, 58-60; wandering mind in, 43-44. *See also* formal mindfulness practices

Mindfulness-Based Stress Reduction (MBSR), 3, 203

Mitteldorf, Bruce, 5

modified cobra pose, 101

modified triangle pose, 129

mountain pose, 122

movement, mindful, 207

N

National Institute of Mental Health, 3

neck stretch, 125

negative interpretations, 56-57

negative self-talk, 54-55, 57

Nelson, Portia, 109-110

neural plasticity, 31

neuroscience, 27, 28

neutral sensations, 69

Nhat Hanh, Thich, 17, 151, 179

nonjudgment, 42

nonlocality theory, 170

nonstriving, 42, 186

norepinephrine, 27

O

Oliver, Mary, 1-2, 199

one-arm stretch, 123

online programs, 203-204

Opening to You: Zen-Inspired Translations of the Psalms (Fisher), 150

openness, 160

Ornish, Dean, 184

P

pain: emotional, 61, 71; investigating, 70; physical, 69-72; practicing mindfulness of, 72

"Painful Case, A" (Joyce), 65

parasympathetic nervous system, 28

parent-child relationships, 158-159

pelvic rock and tilt, 96

physical pain, 69-72; emotions and, 70-71; investigating tension and, 70; present-moment awareness and, 71

planning your practice, 7, 23, 192-194

poetry, 208

pose of openness, 106

practice log, 7, 24

present-moment awareness, 71

prone leg stretch, 101

published resources, 204-206

Q

Quantum Theory (Bohm), 170

R

Rahula, Walpola, 15

RAIN practice, 116

redirection, 167

reflecting on informal practice, 25

relationships: difficult people in, 173; interpersonal patterns in, 157-160, 168-169; mindfulness in important, 169-170; overcoming fear in, 169; work- based, 171-172. *See also* interpersonal mindfulness

relaxation vs. meditation, 32-33

resilience, 109-110

resistance: to connection, 185-186; to exercising, 181-182; to loving-kindness, 150; to rest, 183

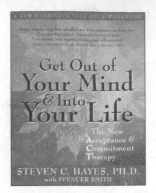